Praise for *Amazing Grace*

"You will be greatly fascinated and encouraged by the wonderful stories of God's amazing grace . . . Wes pulls no punches . . . You will identify with many of the trials Wes and Lori have faced and have more faith that God will also pull you through!"

—Dr. John Benefiel
Sr. Pastor, Church on the Rock, Oklahoma City OK
Chairman, Heartland Apostolic Prayer Network

"Like a cool cup of water on a hot summer day Wes Lane's new book is refreshing! Wes and his helpmate, Lori, are the real deal in a fake world. Everyone should invest the time in reading, no *studying* this book. You will be inspired, challenged, and encouraged through this book."

—Dr. Scott Dawson
Scott Dawson Evangelistic Association

"Wes Lane . . . is refreshingly transparent as he invites us into his life. Wes gives a glimpse of the inner chambers of a district attorney's life as he discusses the several high-profile trials with which he was personally involved. While getting the inside scoop on those trials, Wes also takes you on an odyssey as he journeys towards spiritual maturity. His book was, at times, like reading a good detective novel, and at other times like reading the story of a character in the Bible—with sins and shortcomings out in the open for all to read, while God chisels away on his soul. Anyone who reads this book will find themselves challenged to look into their own life's journey while enjoying Wes's light-hearted humor along the way."

—Bill R. Day
Preacher, Northwest Church of Christ, Oklahoma City OK

"Wes Lane calls himself a 'recovering skeptic' about God, and his humility resounds throughout this book about his life as a husband, prosecutor, and man of faith. His lesson is a simple and profound one: we can't go it alone. His Christian faith is his anchor, and it shows on every page."

—Mary Fallin
Oklahoma Congresswoman

"I was totally captivated by the way you wove extremely interesting court cases around your life story and the insights God has been teaching you on the Christian life. I love the way you paint word pictures and describe truths in ways that I have never heard before. You have an amazingly creative writing style and a grasp of human nature which is refreshingly explained through your transparent self-portrait. I thoroughly enjoyed the book."

—Bill Gothard
Founder and President, Institute for Basic Life Principles

"Amazingly Graced is a transparent journal of one man's life of finding faith out of doubt. Wes Lane is respected and loved by many for his consistent example of living in the light of God's purpose and plan. He followed Christ at first from afar, through some of the normal transitions of life, ending up wholly committed to the life of Christ follower, a place he might not have imagined himself just years earlier. His honest recounting of struggles and difficulties gives us mortals hope that our own path might be that of overcomers in the long term. My confidence is that many will be encouraged, challenged and blessed by reading this autobiography of life and faith."

—Dr. Loren Gresham
President, Southern Nazarene University

"Amazingly Graced is a beautifully transparent picture of Wes Lane's journey from skepticism to the reality of a victorious supernatural life. His humility and authenticity bleed off the page . . . Through his story, he reveals a heartfelt journey to truth, hope, and confidence in a faithful King. Lane will motivate you to join him on the adventure of bringing glory to our Creator by fulfilling His destiny for your life."

—Craig Groeshel
Senior Pastor, LifeChurch.tv, Oklahoma

"Wes Lane's journey is honest, thought-provoking, at times raw, and always interesting. I found myself talking about the book long after I'd read it, to anybody that would listen. Wes's voice for the spiritually hungry is extremely satisfying."

—Rene Gutteridge
Novelist, *Never the Bride* (Random House)

"Your book . . . is wonderful. I couldn't put it down . . . It was an inspiration . . . I heard God in your book. I can't wait for it to be published."

—Kim Henry
First Lady, State of Oklahoma

"This is a book about growing a faith that makes a real difference. It's a true story that is packed with high courtroom drama, humor, radical life changes, miraculous healings, and everyday struggles—all experienced on a public stage. Wes has shared his life with deep candor and honesty, creating a great read with a worthy purpose. You'll turn pages in a hurry to find out the rest of the story and cheer as Wes and Lori stay the course, regardless of circumstances. Finally, you'll finish the book inspired and praising a God who is bigger than any problem."

—Jane Jayroe
Miss America 1967, former News Anchor,
former Oklahoma Cabinet Secretary of Tourism,
Co-author of "More Grace than Glamour."

"A very revealing account of Wes Lane's journey from his faith having little or no part in his life to the point where his faith has blossomed into a full-fledged personal relationship with God. An inspirational book for the new Christian, the mature Christian, and everyone in-between."

—Diane Leonard Koch
Widow of Don Leonard, U.S. Secret Service,
killed in Oklahoma City Bombing

"Wes Lane's life and message is a reminder that there is no line between the 'sacred' and the 'secular.' Jesus wants everything and all of us, not just ten to noon on Sundays. All of life is subject to His Kingdom. Wes has seen first-hand that God has not changed. The radical call to come and follow, that Jesus gave to fisherman in the first century is the same call He gives today."

—Josh Kouri
Lead Pastor, Frontline Church, Oklahoma City OK

"Amazingly Graced is a well written, behind the scenes look into how the hand of God sorts through the stories that make the news and the halls of government to change the lives of individuals. As you journey through this book, you will smile, grimace, weep, and celebrate the reality of God's presence. Wes Lane has offered us a no holds barred, authentic, and transparent look at what it means to have your faith challenged, beaten down, stressed to the breaking point, and then emerge more real and powerful than ever before. If you want to be encouraged, enlightened, and edified, read this book!"

—Dr. Dennis Newkirk
Senior Pastor, Henderson Hills Baptist Church, Edmond OK

"Wes Lane may no longer be a prosecutor, but he has made a compelling case 'beyond a reasonable doubt' for why and how Christians can trade our lives of quiet mediocrity for a lives of abundance in Christ. By sharing his personal story of doubt and self-reliance, he has shown us how we mortals can walk the journey—sometimes painful, sometimes joyful—to active faith and complete trust, going far beyond the limitations of our intellectual acknowledgement of our creator and God. You cannot read this book without your life being enriched and changed."

—Mike E. O'Neal
President, Oklahoma Christian University

"Wes Lane has written a masterpiece in "Amazingly Graced." The story of God's grace and one man's struggle to make sense of life come together in this thrilling book. Set in the high pressure world of murder trials and the worst of the human condition we see God connect with a lonely and discouraged man. This inspiring narrative keeps you on the edge of your chair. Written in a vulnerable and compelling style it should be read by all men. I am not sure if women should read it!"

Dr. Ralph Palmen
President, Pinnacle Forum America

"The heart and passion of Wes jumps off the pages and bleeds compassion and faith. I could not put the manuscript down, and came away challenged at a very deep level to believe God more and to see life and God's eternal purposes through the eyes of faith. So, hold on to your seat because this book will rocket you into the orbit of trusting God to show Himself supernaturally in your life each day."

—**Jerry Regier**
Founder, Family Research Council
and former Oklahoma Cabinet Secretary

"Wes Lane's story—from spiritual skepticism to spiritual faith—and how that faith sustained him during his tumultuous days as Oklahoma City District Attorney—is an encouraging account of how God pursues us and then strengthens us once we turn our will over to His will for our lives."

—**Alan E. Sears**
President, CEO & General Counsel,
Alliance Defense Fund

"The most interesting and enlightening books for me are those that, like Amazing Grace, are woven from a person's real-life journey. If truth doesn't work in the everyday grind, it probably isn't truth at all. This book is fascinating, poignantly written, and instructional—a rare mix. You're gonna like this book!"

—**Dutch Sheets**
Bestselling author and Senior Pastor, Freedom Church,
Colorado Springs CO

"People often ask where God is in the midst of hatred and destruction. He is there through His people like Wes Lane who didn't choose to be. He was ordained to be. Whoever accepts great responsibility also accepts the headwinds and the obstacles—the calling comes with opposition. Still, once you have been, as Wes says, 'ruined for the ordinary,' you will know that God upholds those who serve Him in the places of pressure, corruption, pride, and deceit. This is a not a story of a great man but a great story of God's grace."

—**Fred Smith**
President, The Gathering

"Lane gives us a riveting true portrayal of the trials and tribulations of his climb to celebrated prosecutor and big city district attorney. Among many others, his having successfully prosecuted one the most notorious mass murderers of our time, Lane lets us see through his eyes the cold realities a man experiences when he faces the truth of his convictions, fears, anxieties, victories and defeats in the courtroom and through the public family notoriety that comes with running for elected office. He effectively demonstrates for his readers through the web of his ultra-challenging circumstances the faith, climb, and walk of a man who, beginning as skeptic, has been nurtured, honed, and chiseled into a man after God's own heart."

—**Steve Trice**
President and CEO, Jasco Products Co.
Chairman, CBMC/USA, CBMC/Oklahoma City

"Wes Lane is a man of courage and compassion. He is a man of great faith and devout commitment to his family. This incredible book will take you on a journey of 'spiritual warfare' and criminal prosecution. This inspirational and uplifting story is a testimony to the power of prayer and the fact that you just can't keep a GOD MAN down."

—**Mike Turpen**
Former Oklahoma Attorney General

AMAZINGLY
GRACED

AMAZINGLY
GRACED

A TRUE STORY

A PROSECUTOR JOURNEYS THROUGH FAITH,
MURDER, AND THE OKLAHOMA CITY BOMBING

WES LANE

WinePressPublishing
Your Book, Defined. Since 1991.

WinePress Publishing (PO Box 428, Enumclaw, WA 98022) functions only as book publisher. As such, the ultimate design, content, editorial accuracy, and views expressed or implied in this work are those of the author.

Unless otherwise indicated, Scripture quotations are taken from the *New King James Version* of the Bible.

All proceeds from the sale of this book go to the Burbridge Foundation, an organization dedicated to encouraging Christians to be salt and light to their communities.

ISBN 13: 978-1-60615-029-0
ISBN 10: 1-60615-029-4
Library of Congress Catalog Card Number: 2009938346

For my beloved Lori. Thank you for the best years of my life.

Men shall speak of the might of Your awesome acts,
And I will declare Your greatness
—Psalm 145:6

CONTENTS

PREFACE

I was a career prosecutor, trying and convicting some of the most notorious criminals of our community, dealing with evidence day in and day out. This is my "testimony" or, as they say, my "evidence." I now take the stand. This is a book about what I have observed to be an unchanging and amazingly loving, faithful God. It wasn't my idea to write this. In fact, there is a part of me that is somewhat embarrassed what with all the personal information pouring out on these pages, when I was really just trying to share what to me were some surprising observations about God. It seems many people want to pen a book about themselves these days, or believe they need to write such a book, as though the multitude is actually waiting on such a work with grand anticipation. I suffer no such delusion.

That is not to say that some autobiographical works are not important or indeed very interesting and worthy. Certainly there are many. Some folks actually are fascinating in that they have accomplished remarkable things or lived truly impactful lives. Not placing myself in either of those grand categories, this book started out as a simple attempt to share Someone else's story I have found fascinating. Yet, as I sought to tell the story, I found myself forced to relate scenarios that, whether I liked it or not, involved me and my wife, Lori. Invariably we get dragged into the narrative as God's amazing activity was always in connection with our own, at times, public life situation. Consequently, and to my minor discomfort, I found the more I tried to share a story about God, the more I found it impossible to do so without it being within the context of our experience with him. We were inextricably intertwined. So please don't confuse me with the proverbial Hollywood producer who, upon finishing a windy and self-focused tale, finally turns to his bleary-eyed listener and says, "Well, enough about me. . . . What do you think of me?" This is not meant to be a book about the fascinating subject of me.

To further complicate matters, I am married to a very shy person who I suspect contemplates a Robinson Crusoe desert island experience as maybe not such a bad idea. Throughout my tenure as district attorney, Lori often believed she was getting more than her fair share of attention by virtue of our marriage. "What a privilege it is to be the wife of the district attorney," she would sarcastically lament after another "gotcha" news story detailing her challenges with a prescription drug addiction. So it was with some trepidation that I first mentioned to her that for this to be a meaningful and helpful narrative, it would require utter transparency about some of the things we experienced. To her everlasting credit, Lori knew it had been through our greatest adversities that God appeared in the most magnificent ways. Her immediate deadpan response to my comment was, "Well of course! We don't need another fairy tale." Boy, I love that gal.

Honestly, however, there was once a time I would have received the contents of this book as *exactly* that—another fairy tale by some religious nut. I was once a great scoffer, so smug, so all-knowing. I once considered faith largely irrelevant to life, and viewed God like a pet in a cage I could let out every now and again in hopes he would fetch me something I wanted. Now, after over twenty years of observing God do his rather magnificent thing, I have reached a different verdict.

I am not a theologian. I'm just another guy walking out life like the rest of you. I've walked two very different paths, however—the young adult years of my life ignoring God, with the rest in hot pursuit. I have close friends on many sides of the theological debate, from atheists to agnostics, from evangelical to charismatic to Unitarian to mainline Protestant to Catholic, and all points in between. We are all over the map regarding faith-claims, and some, like me, have held more than one position over the years—from "there is no God" to "He exists but is unknowable" to "God does not do the miraculous today!" to "Yes, he does!" I am deeply grateful for the rich and wonderful relationships I have with all my friends!

I ask my readers to please receive this book for simply what it is—a hopefully humble and transparent eyewitness account of what I have observed to be a supernatural experience. Some of my friends will raise a cynic's eyebrow when I use the word "supernatural," but I have been an eyewitness for far too long under too many conditions to "tone down" what I have seen and experienced. Ultimately, you will be the judge.

I hope this account encourages you all, my dear friends. There is both purpose and profound hope out there, and I wrote this book to bring these to you.

—Wes Lane

ACKNOWLEDGMENTS

Asking people to both read my draft manuscript *and* lend criticism was asking a lot. I did so with a number of people and am deeply grateful that several were able to take the time to do both. Heaven knows I did a bunch of deleting and draft massaging after conversations with my critic-friends: Rob Adair, Larry Andrews, Dianne Beffort, Mike Daub, Bill Day, Jane Jayroe Gamble, Mart Green, Rene Gutteridge, Sheila Harder, Sarah Horton, Kent and Davidene Humphreys, Robin Jones, Josh Kouri, Lori Lane, Mom (Bobbie Lane), Phyllis Lane, Julia Loren, Lynne McGuire, Stephanie Pok, Jim Priest, George Rennix, Randy Swanson, Karen Ulman, John and Pat Ward and Anne Wilson (I so hope I didn't leave anyone out). Some of the folks I just mentioned really went above and beyond and I am humbled by their generous efforts.

My editor on the project, Len Goss of GoodEditors.com, was a tremendous help and encouraging guide. I especially want to thank my long time friend (and author) John J. Dwyer. A man prominently mentioned in this book, we continue to ride the trail of life—and faith—together. Thanks "Gil" for your life-long encouragement.

I did not originally include a chapter on the Terry Nichols case. After several reviewers expressed surprise for my not having done so (notably Bill Day who lost his sister, Diana, at the hands of Nichols and

McVeigh), I reconsidered this and am now glad I did. It was personally very meaningful to reflect on that experience in ways I had not before. My thanks to my encouragers, friends, and former co-workers, Sheila Harder, Debbie Forshee, and Stephanie Pok, who spent a long afternoon with me digging through boxes and piles of newspaper articles and other documents related to my dealings with that case. How I have managed not having Sheila and Debbie running my life on a daily basis I do not know! My sincere thanks as well to Suzanne Lister, one of the three intrepid trial prosecutors, for her help in reviewing the chapter draft.

Finally, from the bottom of Lori's heart and mine thank you to all of you who prayed for us during our public experience. Your prayers were marvelously answered!

PART I
THE ALTAR OF SKEPTICISM

When it comes to the question of God, we all have to start some-where. God is willing to address our skepticism, but, being of a gentlemanly nature, he won't force himself upon us if we are determined to not hear the answers to our questions.

CHAPTER ONE

CROWDS OF DOUBT

This prosecution was unjust, unfair, and just plain evil. There was absolutely no way that the beloved John Hamilton, M.D., society OBGYN doctor could possibly have murdered his beautiful wife, Susan. They were the perfect couple, so madly in love, always together, always touching, always perfect. They lived in a well-to-do neighborhood in a lovely home with pristine white floors and tastefully decorated white walls. Theirs was a fairy tale marriage that doubtless most everyone looked at from afar and sighed with romantic, vicarious pleasure. To the public that knew them, the Hamilton's were the cover on a romance novel. When Susan was brutally murdered in her bathroom at home on Valentine's Day, the good doctor was found on the floor on his knees beside her, covered in blood from supposedly trying to save her life. He was absolutely distraught and out of control in his grief. Everybody *knew* he could never have done this. The solidity of skepticism over the truth of his guilt was like reinforced concrete. . . .

The old, ornate metal and glass paneled chandeliers, like the courthouse itself, hearkened back to days of the art deco 1930s. Though they loomed with silent dignity high above the darkly stained woods of the judge's bench and counsel tables, whatever light they brought forth was lost in the vastness of the courtroom. There never seemed quite enough light to me in this old and dignified setting. This judge

1

always kept the tall curtains drawn tightly closed so that the combination of insufficient candle power from the lights and his mysterious unwillingness to allow in a bit of the sun's help, left a murkiness to the room, an aura more befitting a late night poker game than dispensing justice. At least it seemed that way to me. But it was the judge's place of business, not mine. He probably had a good reason, but by the time I entered his courtroom on this particular occasion, I really wouldn't care because the room was packed wall to wall with people who didn't seem to like me very much. Scores of them. Every inch of space in the long and rigid double rows of wooden pews was filled with tightly wedged humans whose every vibe emanated hostility. And since the pews were not enough, the rest of the spectator's area was standing room only, with individuals lined up colorfully along the walls and filling the passages surrounding the carpeted seating area, heads bobbing in determined conversation.

In that spring of 2001, I was an assistant district attorney, having been requested by the Oklahoma City Police Department's homicide detail to be specially assigned to prosecute this immensely high profile murder case. The occasion for the courtroom spectacle was a bond hearing for the eminent, and recently arrested, Dr. John Hamilton, M.D., who was adored by his many patients. I was seeking to keep him in jail and ultimately to send him to prison. To the crowd, I was the enemy.

The separate structures of the Oklahoma County Courthouse and the Oklahoma County Office Building are joined by a breezeway at the fifth floor level. Since the Oklahoma County District Attorney's Office is on the fifth floor of the Office Building, the most common manner of getting over to the courthouse is down the slippery white linoleum slope of the breezeway. It was slippery because the two fifth floors are about a half-floor off from fitting together properly. A couple of more degrees of angle and they would have had to turn it into a stairwell. Over my career I had walked, trotted, and run that path countless times, heading for some courtroom, sometimes with armfuls of files, sometimes with just pen and yellow legal pad in the black plastic covered notebook stamped in gold letters "Assistant District Attorney," sometimes white-knuckling a big piece of rolling audio/

visual equipment down the slick, steep slope, hoping it wouldn't get away from me and run over someone.

There was always something magical about that breezeway to me. Maybe it's the music that plays in your head when you go through it on the way to dispense justice. At least it played for me. I first noticed that tune as a baby lawyer fresh out of law school, a brand new assistant DA, all wet behind the ears, almost clueless on what I was doing. I only knew I was headed off to court to do battle with evil. The tune would start up just after passing the elevators on the fifth floor of the County Building, and continue past the jury room on the left with its summoned citizens milling about, wishing they were anyplace else. It played as you met the center handrail that split the passage descending into the bowels of the courthouse's fifth floor, a place where every accused felon has to pass through on his way to trial like dust through a filtering system. I think maybe the music was the theme from Dragnet. It was almost like a prosecutorial marching theme, the prosecutor's version of "The Battle Hymn of the Republic." The heavy dramatic tune kept time with my every pattering step. It would come with goose bumps too. I felt like I was marching to battle, marching for truth, justice, and the American way. I could at times even see the flag flying in front of me, kind of like on the old Superman television shows where at the end, after Superman had prevailed over the bad guy, there he would stand as the credits rolled by, his cape fluttering in the breeze before the gently waving red, white, and blue. I felt like Superman. I think most prosecutors do. At least maybe the men. I don't know what character of justice female prosecutors feel like. But I figure the guys feel like Superman, or the Lone Ranger, or a noble knight on a white horse. It feels like you're on the side of everything good and right and just. You're saving someone no less than a fireman is saving a person from a burning building, or a knight saves a beautiful girl from a castle tower. Even though it is after the fact, even though the crime has come and gone, you're still "doing justice" for someone, somewhere, and it's bigger than life itself.

The music never really went away. Even when the wet dried behind my ears and a younger lawyer was wrestling equipment down the steep, slippery corridor for me, the music of justice played and played and played.

And so it played on the day I was surrounded by scores of another man's admirers.

The moment I stepped off the elevator onto the seventh floor of the courthouse, my ears were greeted by the low and steady rumble of a crowd's blended voice spilling forth from around the corner at the courtroom's public entrance. I passed that corner and then saw the thick throng milling about the courtroom's double-doored entry, their attention suddenly alert to my appearance causing the great and audible rumble to immediately become hushed. I awkwardly squeezed through the maze of people outside the courtroom and it did not take a mind reader to know how the crowd felt about me. From their vantage point, I was the enemy, the would-be perpetuator of a wonderful and perfect man's demise. I avoided their eyes as best as I could, as there was no point playing games of eye chicken. These folks were not my enemy; at least I didn't think so at that time, as I hadn't received any threats (those would come anonymously later, along with metal detectors for some of the courtroom hearings). The crowd was almost entirely women, and I sensed their tension as my bundle of files and I swam through their midst, past the brimming pews and through the swinging, waist high wooden gate that led to that pretense of sanctuary—the counsel tables and what is known as the "well" of the courtroom.

His supporters came by their skepticism over his guilt honestly, however. They did not know the *facts* of the murder; they only knew what they wanted to believe. I could neither blame them for their animosity nor fail to admire them for their loyalty. It was, I suppose, important to them to believe in this man. Many of these individuals were his patients who only knew him as a kind and soft spoken man. They had never experienced him otherwise, and could in no way picture him strangling and beating his wife to death. To do otherwise would rock their belief system surrounding him. To them, they already *knew* the truth.

Yet, on the general subject of skepticism, I could actually identify with them.

CHAPTER TWO

I THINK I AM IN
LOVE WITH ME

I am a recovering skeptic. About God.

At one time I would never have described myself as such, what with me going to church so much as a kid.

In pondering my "recovering" status, the question popped into my head, What if there existed AA meetings for skeptics? In other words, meetings for folks to go and get help "staying off" God-skepticism. If you have never been to an AA (Alcoholics Anonymous) or NA (Narcotics Anonymous) meeting, these are essentially support groups designed to aid substance abusers in their quest to stay away from drugs and alcohol. There is a lot of coffee drinking, fellowship, personal testimony, encouragement, even a little teaching perhaps—all with a view toward debunking the addictive myth that drugs and alcohol are necessary to cope with life. The goal is to be drug and alcohol free. Period. Certainly relapse is considered part of recovery, but the goal is to pick oneself up again and, one day at a time, never to dabble in substance abuse again.

Briefly, I wondered what such a meeting for recovering skeptics about God would look like—an "SA" (Skeptics Anonymous) meeting, I suppose. Then I realized it would probably look a lot like Sunday church. At church we gather . . . drink coffee . . . fellowship . . . have a meeting in the form of a church service at which our addiction to skepticism

5

about God is supposedly whittled down to size. After this, we leave all pumped up, ready to try believing for another week that God exists, is really interested in us and is relevant to our circumstances. We depend upon the meetings to help us hang in there until the next meeting. One day at a time with occasional relapses. Sort of like an AA meeting.

Except then I realized that at an AA meeting, the thought that drugs or alcohol are *sort of* okay is absolutely unthinkable. On the other hand, the church, to varying degrees, often seems to welcome shades of doubt and unbelief—i.e. skepticism—about God and what he is up to in our world. At times, skepticism is subtly appreciated and cultivated in church. Sometimes it is even preached! I say "subtly appreciated" because I've noticed that at many churches there is a lot of preaching about an omnipotent God but there are great undercurrents of skepticism about how active that supposedly omnipotent God is willing to be in our lives. It is as though we want to believe God is almighty, but because we have not personally experienced him in our circumstance, it is easier to just believe he is more "God-lite." In other words, we maintain a very low expectation level regarding his supernatural involvement in our situation. We feel a cathartic benefit for having prayed, but take out an insurance policy to cover our nagging doubts concerning whether he will actually take the time to get involved.

Which is probably why we have a lot of relapse into heavy skepticism between the meetings.

I'm not sure exactly how I became a skeptic about God. I hadn't always thought of myself as such. I would have envisioned a God-skeptic looking the professorial type with thick glasses; an existential individual hanging out unshaven in French cafés contemplating deep thoughts about the futility of life while swirling a glass of red wine.

I, on the smug other hand, "believed" in God.

It ruined everything for me when I looked up the definition in Merriam-Webster's®:

> Skepticism: 1: an attitude of doubt or a disposition to incredulity either in general or toward a particular object; 2a: the doctrine that true knowledge or knowledge in a particular area is uncertain b: the method of suspended judgment, systematic doubt, or criticism characteristic

of skeptics; 3: doubt concerning basic religious principles (as immortality, providence, and revelation) synonyms see UNCERTAINTY[1]

I hated that definition. It described me right on the nose. I was, it would appear, an active skeptic. What's more, I found myself feeling rather fashionable when I would raise a knowing eyebrow of unbelief now and then upon hearing someone claim that God had done something somewhat, well, supernatural. Unless, of course, that person was a missionary giving testimony concerning events taking place in a third world country far, far away. For some reason, at least for me, it was somehow okay to believe God did something rather omnipotent if it was in the jungle.

Perhaps my skepticism is the psychological part of why I became a lawyer. As lawyers, we don't hear a story from someone without raising a knowing eyebrow and wondering how much of what we are being told is actually the truth. We are always saying things like, "Show me the evidence!" or "Prove it to me!" We're big on skepticism, unless, of course, we are talking about our client and our case.

I am not sure anyone is born a skeptic; we just arrive there somehow. As I reflect back, I can see that God had to do a few things to take me from "skeptic" to "recovering skeptic." My goal is to get out of recovery completely, but that will involve zero relapses ever again and that very thought overwhelms me. Still, it is my goal. One day at a time. At least I came by my skepticism in the usual way.

I Wish I Was Cool

I was born and raised in Oklahoma City. My father, after whom I am named, did not really "fall in love" with Jesus until he was in his forties, long after my sister, Dianne, and I had flown the nest to go off to college. Like many, his early experience with religion was more guilt-based than lovingly relational. As a kid he was always getting into trouble. He was, after all, a pastor's kid and for some mysterious reason that often seems to be a tailor made environment for a young person wanting to take a walk on the wild side. Certainly my dad did. He was constantly getting caught with a pack of playing cards, going to movies, or engaging in some sort of activity considered sinful in the denomination in which he was being raised. With his father passing away when Dad was a mere three years old, and being the ninth of nine kids, his mother doubtless had her hands full. He finally considered himself a lost cause for faith at an early age, what with having to "go forward" so often on altar calls to repent. He just gave up on God completely. He figured he could never be good enough. Were he alive today, I am confident he would admit that as a young twenty-something year old man, the sole reason he started attending First United Methodist Church in downtown Oklahoma City back in the early 1950s was to check out the girls.

It was at this church that he met and married my mother, then Bobbie Jean Burbridge. Mom was a devout nineteen year old when they married, but as is so often the case when lovers marry, the lower common religious denominator ultimately drags the other down to their level instead of the reverse. Dad was at all the church events as they dated and salesman that he was, managed to convince my attractive mother that he was as interested in God as she was. As it turned out, after they married his interest in the things of God severely waned and it became a real point of conflict in their increasingly turbulent marriage.

Regardless of their conflict about faith and each other, they loved my sister and me and wanted our very best. For some reason, despite his personal conflict with God, both of our parents believed it important that my sister and I attend church. Dad was just an infrequent visitor himself and his routine absence was exasperating to his young and pious wife (Dad told me often how early in their marriage he would observe her on her knees praying).

Sunday mornings were a continuing source of marital conflict, as I remember that oft asked embarrassing question coming at my mother as she would arrive at church alone with us—"Where's Big Wes?" The totality of that struggle with my father ultimately took its toll, wearing her down to the point where not long before their divorce when I was twelve and my sister nine, her own relationship with God was on the wane. Dad's at times vehement antagonism with Christianity ultimately pulled Mom up off her knees. I am pleased to say that years later, both of them found, or re-found in my mother's case, their way to vibrant relationships with God. But, as is usually the case, the Bible has a point when it speaks to an issue, in this instance the challenging matter of being "unequally yoked."[2]

Regarding our church life, my sister and I had the advantage of being exposed to great teaching and strong biblical fundamentals at the independent Baptist church we attended, Metropolitan Baptist. We understood the basics of the Christian faith *intellectually*, but unfortunately, this is largely where it stopped for me. Although I told Jesus I was "his guy" at a very young age, accepting Christ as my Savior at the assistance of my also devout maternal grandmother, Velma Jean Burbridge, somehow, someway there was a disconnect between that intellectual understanding and coming to regard God as a loving heavenly Father that wanted to be deeply relevant to every aspect of my life.

Thus, I really don't remember thinking much about God outside of the church walls as a little kid. I could recite a single verse—John 3:16, "For God so loved the world that he gave his only Son, that whoever believes in him shall not perish but have eternal life." Even now I can type that verse from memory from those days. But really, it didn't mean much to me then. I could also count to ten in French.

My maternal grandfather, R.O. Burbridge, used to drive me crazy making me recite either that verse or those French numbers to every stranger he'd run into at the coffee shop he would frequent. "Wessie, speak some French to the man!" I wanted to evaporate. French numbers or Bible verses were all about the same to me. He also had me sticking Christian tracts in phone booths. It was very embarrassing.

Looking back, I know my parents did not mean for me to have a shallow relationship with God during my childhood. They both grew up in strong Christian homes, and actually in the long run they did a great deal to influence my sister and me with that early foundational church experience. But at a young age, it just seemed to break down somewhere along the line between the *teaching* of God and the *experience* of God in my day-to-day circumstances. There was a great deal of the former from church, but virtually none of the latter. Consequently, I was never quite sure why God was relevant at all (a great seed bed for youthful skepticism). I did not have any close relationships of a mentoring nature with anyone having a vibrant relationship with God, so I saw a lot of religious activity but no real spiritual power.

To make matters worse, I was a raging nerd.

I was very shy as a little boy. I know Dad was worried about me. I suspect it partly stemmed from the time I brought home the G.I. Joe doll that was all the rage in the mid-1960s. "Boys don't play with [double expletive deleted] dolls!" he exploded. I remember the moment to this day. My parents were still married at the time and we were having one of those "Norman Rockwell" evenings. We were gathered in our book lined den which we called "the library". The previous owners had left hundreds of books on the shelves upon their departure and had someone stumbled upon us that evening they would have doubtless thought us voracious readers. The big black and white T.V. inside the fine wooden cabinet was in an exalted position at one end of the room, opposite the screened fireplace at the other. There was an old painting of some obscure nature scene looming above us on the mantle in an ornate gold frame. Mom was sitting in the fancy leather reclining chair beneath a bright lamp, intently focused on a pile of knitting in her lap and giving the task at least a nominal try (it didn't last much beyond that night—she shared with me she still has the same Mohair yarn and knitting needles in a closet somewhere). Dad was sitting on our old green cloth sofa. He had brought home a new cigarette he was trying. These were filled with fragrant pipe tobacco so he was pretending to read the newspaper but really blowing his smoke around the room hoping we would notice its supposedly savory aroma. Who wouldn't notice? The smoke billowed intermittently up and over his paper like smoke signals. With the output, one would have thought Dad was on fire or something. I don't know where my little sister was at the time. Probably rooting through mom's makeup drawer or playing dolls somewhere.

I, on the other hand, was sitting on the rug at my parents' feet, unwrapping the days T.G.&Y. store purchase of the much coveted "G.I. Joe." I was in prepubescent ecstasy. Every Saturday morning I would wake up early, grab a blanket and pillow to go downstairs and lay before the big T.V., transfixed watching cartoons. On commercial breaks, the air waves would erupt with happy boys playing war with their G.I. Joe dolls (my own son, years later, would become very indignant when I deviously called his X-men "dolls" to get a rise out of him—*"They're action figures!"* he would always retort. Some things never change.). So, after a steady diet of those Saturday morning commercials, I had to have that toy! Not being particularly stupid, I also knew which of my parents I could prevail upon with sufficient whining to get it for me—Mom.

And so, ensconced in our happy domestic scene, I excitedly unwrapped my package, revealing my plunder. Dad, peering from around his paper to see if anyone's nostrils had finally detected his own exciting purchase, leveled his eyes casually upon his name sake, gradually settling upon what was in his progeny's grubby little hands. The newspaper came crashing down to his lap and he sat momentarily in stunned disbelief. Now Dad was a manly sort of fellow. He wasn't into sports or hunting or things like that but, still, he was firmly opposed to all things sissy and I had heard him make disdainful comments about those "queers" before. I suspect his mind was already frantically extrapolating from my hands holding onto a doll to the abysmal, ghastly, man's man nightmare of his very own seed someday holding another man's hand with Sodom and Gomorrah-ish intent. Dad started to smoke without the cigarette. It was then that the double expletive eruption took place.

My mother, of course, quickly came to my defense and for a moment there was a chilling standoff in the room. My eyes must have been as big as saucers as I quickly and quietly pretended G.I. Joe had evaporated or had otherwise been rendered invisible. My mind raced on how to change the subject. It was then that I made a major blunder in my kid's effort at diplomacy. I turned to Mom, pointed at her knitting and innocently asked, "Hey, Mom, could you show me how to do that?"

One would have thought Dad had been sitting in the ejection seat of James Bond's Astin-Martin race car by the way he exploded off of that sofa, uttering choice epithets, and pounding out of the room, fragrant cigarette smoke plume trailing in his wake.

Dad was very, very worried.

I have a very strong suspicion that this was why my dad would actually let me go to school in the sixth grade carrying a briefcase and having the old plastic "pocket protector" in my shirt pocket (for the younger generation of readers, that was a receptacle nerds slid into their shirt pockets to keep pencils and pens from staining their shirt). I don't have the faintest idea who had the original thought of teaming me up with a briefcase and pocket protector, but for some reason I still thought I looked pretty sharp with them and the little uniform eighth grade and younger boys had to wear at Casady School—white or blue Oxford button down shirts, khaki pants, penny loafers and white socks.

To make matters worse, I was badly nearsighted and wore black horn rimmed glasses with coke bottle lenses. I think Dad must have purposefully set me up for character developing opportunities because between the briefcase, pocket protector, and nerd glasses I might as well have hung a sign on my back stating, "Please beat me up." And the other boys pretty much did just that. Even the fifth graders would hunt me down for sport. Back then the school's play ground was like a sort of Darwinian testing ground, survival of the fittest—at least as far as it would go at a private Episcopal school in the 1960s. Small packs of boys would hunt straggling nerds like lions stalking a gimpy gazelle. The purpose of this grand exercise was to subject their victim to "the pole treatment." It was all rather innocent actually—remember, it was a time that "Ozzie and Harriett" was still on the air. The nerd, on the other hand, probably took a dimmer view on the game as he ran frantically from the others until they cornered him, dragged him over to the flagpole where a boy would grab each leg, spread his legs wide and run that vital area up against the flag pole at warp speed. Thank God they never caught me. I might have been a nerd, but I was a fast one.

Racking one another was quite the rage at that age. I have no idea why. It just was. I remember stepping out of a crowded vestibule coming out of a classroom when I saw this kid named Dale come up to me. I liked Dale, he was a nice guy, the fastest guy in the middle school except for Raymond, but I'd lost count of how many times Raymond had flunked and been held back a grade. The kid was probably driving a car to sixth grade, so he really didn't count for speed. Suddenly I saw Dale's right leg swing back and then, like the soccer player he was, his right foot swiftly and with tremendous accuracy connected with my groin. I dropped like a sack of potatoes. Then, another kid named Jackie, immediately jumped on my dazed, pain stricken back as I lay face down against the cold cement and began to poke me in the damaged area as he mindlessly tittered, "Scrounge, scrounge" to the crowd.

What was that about? "Scrounge, scrounge?" My medical doctor wife tells me that boys undergo some sort of acid wash in our brains in the womb. She is of the opinion that men have had half their brains eaten away from the process and are thus demented from birth. What can I say? Jackie later went to prison for armed robbery, which was pretty low rent for a Casady graduate. If a fellow went to prison after having attended a fine college prep school like Casady, you would expect it to be for major financial fraud or something more criminally polished. Dale, the guy who place kicked my testicles, later became a financial contributor to one of my election campaigns, so I forgave him.

I wanted to be cool so very badly. I think this was probably why I was ultimately so highly qualified to run the DA's juvenile division decades later. At least to some degree, I understood the delinquent mind, which is to say I had a profound understanding of the depth of stupid to which a boy could stoop. I was willing to do the most senseless things to be accepted.

I started running around a little with another kid named Cody. At least he sort of paid attention to me until he got kicked out of Casady. He thought it was cool to smoke grape vines. We had a wild grape vine at home so I would bring short, dried vines to school in a metal band aid box and we would light up in the sixth grade boy's bathroom. They would burn the fool out of our tongues. But still, it was the riskiest thing I ever did in my life up to that point. I felt downright dangerous, which was as close to cool as I was going to get. These were pretty small bathrooms and just outside the classroom doors so we weren't exactly the brightest twelve year old bulbs on the Christmas tree. Still, I wanted to be accepted, like every other kid on the block, but the combination of major geekdom and super shyness pretty much hamstrung my grade school potential for greatness in the popularity department.

On the other hand, high school started opening life up to me a bit. Those youthful male hormones kicked in, I got contact lenses, and at sixteen I drove a fancy Mustang Mach I and started seeing girls. I really thought I was making some headway until one evening I made the mistake of smugly sharing at the dinner table how so many girls seemed *very* interested in me. It was at that point that my mouthy little sister let me in on one of the mysteries of the universe. *"Oh dummy,"* she seethed through her braces, *"they just like you for your car!"* She said it with great and disdainful relish. I think she was still smarting over how many years earlier I had duped her into thinking the bathroom sink was a wishing well and had almost managed to abscond with all of her pennies but for unfortunate parental intervention. In any event, I was stunned at my sister's revelation! She said it with a knowing feminine authority, like she was betraying a dark secret. A part of me was forced to believe her. Not only was being "cool" and "accepted" tough enough for me, apparently I could only attain it with the aid of accessories.

By the time I left for college, whatever very nominal relationship I had with God pretty much went out the window. He just wasn't all that popular.

I recall having only one single college conversation—maybe thought—about God during the entire four years (maybe even seven if you count law school). I was sitting in the dining room of my University of Oklahoma fraternity house, Delta Tau Delta (which was a marvelous group of men, by the way, although I did disparagingly refer to the fraternity's few overt Christians as the "God Squad") having a conversation with my then roommate, Mark. We were discussing God for some strange reason and I distinctly recall making a comment to the effect, *"Yeah, I guess I believe in that God stuff. Maybe when I get old I'll get into that . . ."*

Today I look back and am so grateful that God is Patience Personified. And what on earth did I mean when I said *"I believe"*? I *believed* that if I touched a hot stove I would be burned. Had I actually *believed* in God, however, then there would have been a very different set of collegiate behaviors. I can only figure that sitting at that fraternity dining table waxing all philosophic that I was actually just lying my socks off. Or if I wasn't lying perhaps I was just in utter rebellion. In either event I was playing the skeptic, all-knowing and aloof in my twenty-year-old smugness. But, on the other hand, at least we were having a *conversation* about God. I think God is a lot nicer than I used to think. I don't think he was getting all steamed up listening to our conversation, contemplating loosing a thunderbolt my way. I think he was smirking and shaking his head. He already knew the game plan and that I was a hard head. He had dealt with my type before. Don't you know God must have heard his wayward kids say some of the stupidest things over the centuries?

Unfortunately for the state of my skepticism, my one clear memory of interacting with "Christians" in college was when I waited on a party of them while working as a waiter at a restaurant called "The Fox & Horn." Actually, I did not even know they considered themselves to be Christians until they left. As you know, waiters make their money on tips. No tip, no income. When the moment came for me to check out the tip tray, instead of cash there was this tiny little booklet with the picture of a quarter on it. Period. No money. I couldn't believe it. I picked up the little booklet which was about the size of a medium size post-it note. On the cover above the picture of the quarter was the caption "Here is a Tip." Cute. I opened the booklet up and it told me that Jesus loved me and died for my sins. Of course I was immediately convicted, dropped to my knees right in front of the other tables and cried out to God for forgiveness.

Not hardly.

What I was actually thinking that night about those folks I cannot now type as I don't cuss anymore. Or at least I try hard not to.

The dining evangelists made the mistake that so many of us make. At least I have. I get so consumed with *my* thing that I forget that when I am trying to reach other people that I am supposed to be interested in *their* thing also. Lori says I did that to her when we were dating. She claims the experience was something like having a Christian choke hold put on her. I was less interested in how she felt and more into what Christianese she would spout in response to my questions. It was more about form and not so much substance. By that time (I was thirty-two) I was all immersed in church and walking a different life, the reasons for which I'll explain later. I would quiz Lori about the finer points of biblical doctrine to see if she really "believed" in God (as if her head knowledge would prove something). She, on the other hand, just wanted to kill me (in Christian love of course). I have since repented of that and try not to cram God down people's throats. I think they are less likely to throw him up that way.

To be honest, I don't think that if the dining evangelists left me a one hundred dollar bill beneath their tract that I would have repented that night, either. But I would have at least given it respect when I read it. Who knows? It could have operated as a good seed instead of a memory weed in my life. And certainly I would not have gone around to the rest of the waiter crew that night showing off the tract, maligning the Christian idiots. Those folks simply did not move their ball downfield that night.

I Am Now Very Cool

It is awfully hard to hear God when the applause is so loud. Especially when you are doing some of your own clapping.

I went on to O.U. law school ultimately starting work my final semester as a legal intern for Bob Macy in January of 1981. When I started work for Mr. Macy, he had only been the Oklahoma County District Attorney for a few months. It was grand excitement for a twenty-five year old, hanging out at a real courthouse, helping on real cases, dealing with real law instead of law school theories. Blood and guts, cops and robbers. It was a heady experience. After graduating in May, I became an official assistant district attorney on June 1, 1981, which also was my first day in my first trial by myself. We were thrown into the fire quickly in those days.

I think my relationship with Mr. Macy was quickly cemented on a hot summer night shortly after I became a prosecutor. It was "DUI Night." A grand joint operation amongst Oklahoma County law enforcement. We were setting up road blocks on multiple streets looking out for drunk drivers. A handful of "baby" prosecutors, like me, were going to get to ride along with Oklahoma City police and Highway Patrol troopers. Ken, the trooper I was riding with that evening, came to pick me up at my Mother's house where I was living at the time. The times being such as they were, nobody thought twice about the trooper loaning me my complimentary loaded pistol and handcuffs. Folks of that era did not live in civil suit paranoia over an untrained, young, more brawn-than-brains prosecutor being armed and dangerous. I was in tall cotton (for non-southerners that means I was "livin' the dream")! It was several hours later patrolling on I-35 that we pulled behind a weaving drunk driver, and the chase was on. It was rather surrealistic.

As I glanced over at the speedometer spiking out at well over 100 miles per hour, I remember wondering where I should stick my pistol since I didn't have a holster. Do I put it in my belt or my pants or even my pocket? Before I had the opportunity to sort that out, we screamed off onto a darkened side road, lights flashing and siren blaring. The drunk swung into a gravel lot where it suddenly skidded to a stop. Ken and I jumped out of our respective doors, guns drawn, and even an experienced observer would have believed that I was actually trained for this stuff. I remember joining Ken in yelling *Freeze!* or something official like that. Suddenly, a passenger popped out of the car and the driver sped away and "I'm-gonna-live-forever" assistant D.A. Wes yells out "I've got him, Ken!" Ken, actually believing that I meant what I said, jumped back into his car and peeled out of the pitch black parking lot, leaving me alone with a slobbering drunk.

Fortunately for the citizens of Oklahoma County I had seen every "Dirty Harry" movie in which Clint Eastwood had appeared. Therefore I knew *everything* I needed to know. I commanded him to "Get on your belly!" (I probably sprinkled in some encouraging descriptive language I used to be famous for). Much to my surprise and good fortune—he did! I moved in quickly, telling him to *"spread 'em,"* etc., etc. But then, the critical moment—I wasn't quite sure how to put handcuffs on someone. I had one hand filled with a pistol. The thought crossed my mind, *Hmmm . . . now how had I seen them do that?* I opted for a real Dirty Harry alternative. The drunk lay cursing me face down in the gravel at which point I crammed the muzzle of the pistol into the back of his neck and said the following—which I might add was incredibly effective—"Now you listen, I'm real scared and if you so much as breath I'm gonna blow-your-head-off!" Heaven moved and I swear I don't think that guy took a breath for at least a full minute.

I quickly fumbled around with the handcuffs trying to get them on his hands (this was not going to be as easy as I thought). Without a holster or pocket big enough, I finally just set the pistol down on the ground. Fortunately, I was not with an experienced crook, or if he was, he recognized that my incompetence just might get him shot. The next problem was that I did not know very much about how handcuffs operated and learned that night that if you squeeze those things really good, they will tighten up and inflict a great deal of pain. Oops. I squeezed and he squealed. And kept on squealing, cussing me and slobbering into the rocks. I really didn't know what else to do. Ken had not given me a key.

It seemed like a pretty good wait we had in the darkness of that summer night, with him moaning and mumbling rock-muffled epithets, but after a while I could see off in the distance a long line of tiny squad cars coming my way, their lights and sirens increasingly piercing the darkness as they approached. They pulled up to a stop in front of us and lo and behold! Who should hop out of the second car but my very own boss, Bob Macy! Now my boss was a big, robust, Stetson-and-string-tie wearing ex-cop who made about two of me and I thought the man was going to pop a button out of pride that one of his boys bagged a real live criminal. He came towering up to me and gave me a big and brawny bear hug. I had definitely arrived.

I went on to have two extremely successful years as a prosecutor, but, as I will touch on later, the success only reinforced my growing belief that I was invincible and quite possibly the smartest guy in the world. I have to confess, if I wanted to begin a process by which the rock of my skepticism about God's activity in our lives would start being chipped away, I was setting myself up brilliantly.

The not knowing what I wanted to do with my life informed my ultimate restlessness and, continuing to be on my own personal search for significance, I ended up leaving the district attorney's office the summer of 1983. I had met a girl the year before and married her shortly after my departure. I think we both thought I was going to be a hot shot trial attorney and make a lot of money. I joined the second oldest law firm in Oklahoma City, Looney, Nichols, Johnson and Hayes. But after six months at the firm I just wasn't happy. The men and women at the firm were fine folks but something just was not clicking, and I still did not know what I wanted to do with the rest of my life. I left the firm, dragging my wife along with me on my personal search for significance.

I initially went into business with my dear step-father, Eddie Haynes. Eddie was always more than good to me for which I will always be grateful. He was (and is) a real estate auctioneer and for a time I left the practice of law to go to work for him. My next career lurch took place upon seeing a Famous Amos Cookie Bakeshop while attending a real estate seminar in Memphis, Tennessee. Having eaten those cookies by the pound during law school, when I saw this franchise opportunity I just knew this was the deal that would make me rich.

Eddie warned me. Everybody with a brain warned me. Their message was clear: *"You might have a great idea and the timing might indeed be perfect but you cannot borrow yourself into success."* But I knew better. I was "Wes Lane—Smartest Guy in the World," and nobody was going to presume to instruct me. Surely I could defy gravity. After all, hadn't I won all those trials as a prosecutor? Didn't I have a nice plaque on my wall declaring me a gen-u-ine "WINNER"? I was the real deal. So I borrowed and borrowed and spent and spent, never contemplating that what might have been a good deal for a dollar would not be for ten. I opened two franchise locations, one in Oklahoma City and the other right by the university football stadium in Norman. I built that Norman store despite the fact that another franchise had failed at a similar location in another state. Hey, but did I care? Of course not because I was, again, "Wes Lane—Smartest Guy in the World." (I could almost hear my cape fluttering in the breeze, and see an American flag in the background). Just because college kids would not pay for gourmet cookies in Arizona surely did not mean they would not buy them at my store in Oklahoma. I closed down the store within a couple of years. My arrogance was beginning to reap a heavy price. The Oklahoma City store was doing great, but the debt was too much for the pair. I was in way over my head. My income had gone from steady to zilch. My wife left me and the financial roller coaster in October of 1984. We had been married just over a year. I had not given her much to hope for.

So Much for Cool

Pride has always been my Achilles heel. I have learned that God does have some thoughts on the matter. In the fall of 1984, I was getting a lot of the wrong messages from folks concerning my marital separation. They appealed to my pride with lines like: "It's not right!" "It's not fair!"

"What will people think?" or "You need to file for divorce before she does!" After all, it wasn't like I was having an affair with another woman. Pride, pride, ego, ego, and I was buying into it. My family and friends were all singing the same song. Except one. John Dwyer was one of my best friends from college. He was talking Jesus to me. The former college wild man had gone and gotten himself saved! His own life challenges had finally forced the issue a couple of years earlier and Jesus Christ had changed his life. He had been hammering me a bit on the subject over that time, and he even dragged me to a Bible study down in Norman briefly. But still I was really just a God-dabbler. I didn't mind a whiff of God just to hedge my bets, but please, let's not get too serious, shall we? I was the classic guy spoken of by Wilbur Reese:

> $3 Worth of God
> I would like to buy $3 worth of God, please.
> Not enough to explode my soul or disturb my sleep, but
> just enough to equal a cup of warm milk or a snooze in the
> sunshine.
> I don't want enough of Him to make me love a black man
> or pick beets with a migrant.
> I want ecstasy, not transformation.
> I want the warmth of the womb not a new birth.
> I want about a pound of the eternal in a paper sack.
> I'd like to buy $3 worth of God, please.

Finally I succumbed to the ego propaganda and made an appointment concerning a divorce with a buddy of mine from law school. *Perhaps I should get the jump on her after all,* I thought. But John had another thought. "Would you have lunch with me? I'd like for you to meet somebody." I agreed and was to meet him for lunch with my lawyer appointment for later that afternoon.

We met in a south Oklahoma city restaurant. With John was a man named Wayne Marley. He was about my Dad's age it seemed. It started off easy enough.

"Wes, are you a Christian?" he asked.

"Sure" I responded (hey, this is America, aren't we all?)

"How would you define being a Christian?" he probed.

"A Christian is one who recognizes himself as a sinner in need of a savior and accepts Jesus Christ as such." I was good. I had been to Vacation Bible School.

"Hmmm. That's good. A real textbook response," he replied. All the man needed was a pipe and goatee to stroke.

I don't really remember how much more probing he did. What I do remember was that it was a Divine Moment. I had been roughed up enough over the preceding couple of years that if Dr. Phil had had a show in that era, he would have probably asked me, *So this Wes Lane Smartest Guy in the World concept—how's it workin' for ya?* Obviously not too well. Whereas I might have been a slight reprobate (if there are degrees) as a college guy, as I had gotten older I tended to at least be intellectually honest. If someone asked me an honest question, they would get an honest answer.

As I sat there getting an honest look in Wayne Marley's spiritual mirror, I knew my plan was *not* working at all and that I was a failure. I was living in a dumpy apartment. I was hundreds of thousands of dollars in debt. My wife left me. GMAC was calling because I couldn't make the truck payments. To be truthful, I didn't even *have* a plan much less answer the question *how's it working?* Maybe Wayne Marley sensed that, or the Holy Spirit within him did. He went to the heart of the matter. To me, it was a knock-out blow:

"So Wes, what is it you do? Just tear those pages from the Bible that are inconvenient with your lifestyle?"

I felt like I had just received the full swing of a spiritual baseball bat to my chin. I had so brilliantly failed that I was perfectly set up for just this moment. It all came crashing down. On any other day I would have probably deftly side-stepped the blow, but not that day. The question really left me no place to hide and frankly, maybe I was just plain tired of the game I was playing. There was only one true response and that was *Yes.* Ignoring inconvenient biblical concepts was what I had *always* done. But up to that point I honestly had not cared whether I was ignoring the Bible's printed page or not because I had no real ongoing "relationship" with God anyway. I had only read about him, never experienced him. It had all been something akin to taking a class on "Theory of Your Father 101," but never having actually met the man. I was supposed to take it on good authority somehow that Jesus would somehow impact my life. Well, my life had taken a series of bad turns and I was now at a dead end of my own making. I wish I could relate that God had been my first choice, but in truth, he was my last resort. I was now going to see whether this God was going to impact my life or not.

I have come to believe that God has a tremendous sense of humor. Where did we humans get laughter after all? We are supposed to be made in the Creator's image. I don't hear my dog laugh. My heavenly "Dad" must have gotten a bit of a kick out of me at that moment of decision at the restaurant. I was all gung ho. I made a commitment to Jesus right then and there, or at least I got serious with the one I agreed to as a child. I marched out of there a new man. It was as though I could hear the "Hallelujah Chorus" playing in the background! God's man of action, Wes Lane—S.G.I.T.W. (Smartest Guy in the World), had just made another command decision! I would issue an edict of love to my wife and *surely* all would be well in my marriage. I cancelled the divorce appointment, went to that dumpy apartment and promptly wrote her a letter taken directly from 1 Corinthians 13, the Bible's "love" chapter. I can hear me scratching away even now, pouring out how everything was going to change, including me. I quoted from the verses that love is patient, love is kind . . . etcetera, etcetera.

I knew that everything was going to be great now. I had gotten right with God, so can't we just skip to the end? As I said, God had to be getting a chuckle at my enthusiasm while shaking his head as he had quite an extended trip planned. I might have declared my "trust" in the God of the universe, but the real question was, "could he trust me?" He was not going to let me skip the boot camp portion of my nascent faith (in fact, I don't believe I've ever left; just graduated to different levels). I sent the letter. Suffice it to say, it went nowhere. I thought everything was going to now be heaven. Instead it began months of hell.

But wait a minute! I thought things were supposed to automatically get better once you sign up with God! Unfortunately, it would seem God is in the character development business, and this involves an inconvenient mix of time and pressure. I thought I had signed up for an easy cruise, but as it turned out, I signed up for a demanding and rigorous process of Christian maturation.

There would be no quick fix. Furthermore, just as Humpty Dumpty's men could not put Humpty Dumpty back together again, nor could Wes Lane salvage his marriage. Months of pleading, counseling and tears only resulted in a dead end. I had waited too long to address the cancer growing in my marriage. The patient was dead. I finally agreed to let her attorney brother fill out the necessary paperwork and it was over.

I have observed that unless we are married to someone absolutely crazy, men are largely responsible for the success or failure of a marriage. By that I mean that women seem so very wired for relationship, while we, on the other hand, seem to be wired for everything else. What seems to take less concentration on her part takes total focus from him. Consequently, in the vast majority of marriages I have either observed or counseled, it has clearly been the male who could have stopped the ship of marriage from sinking by lovingly and sacrificially treating his wife as God instructed him, rather than treating her like luggage on his personal voyage to success. I am sure I was no different. I lost my ship. My ex-wife has a lovely family today and I wish her all the best.

But the first time I *experienced* the ultimate reality of God was in the aftermath of that divorce. The first major blow to my skepticism took place *after* I had suffered this grand defeat. This was the first time I was not running my own show, and I was blindly following a new leader. I experienced God because it was the first time I heard him speak to me. Today, I suspect he had probably said some things before, but because I was tuned to the wrong station, the Divine Voice was static to me. In the movie theater parking lot, however, I would hear the voice loud and clear.

The Voice in the Parking Lot

My first *overt experience* of God happened shortly after the divorce. I started attending the church of my childhood. It was rather embarrassing showing up that first Sunday after over a ten-year absence. Plus, my decision to attend the singles Sunday school class made it all the more difficult. I felt like someone who had flunked the couples class and was being sent back to singles for some remedial work. To put things in perspective, keep in mind that I felt like I had been dropped like a proverbial hot potato. Surely most of us have experienced the short end of the stick in our dating lives—the boyfriend or girlfriend who jettisons you for a swifter model. I was no stranger to this. I had experienced at least one major "dumping" in high school when the surprise college boyfriend of my first love and high school sweetheart dropped by my house just to let me know he had stolen her from me. I still wish I had punched him (did I write that?). But the real blow to my machismo was that he looked like some frail, long-haired Woodstock loser out of the hippie movement. Maybe I didn't pop him out of my sheer shock that I had been snookered by *this* guy. At any rate, most of us know that yucky, miserable feeling in the pit of our stomachs that comes from blatant love rejection.

After months of utter misery as I futilely sought to rekindle my wife's affection, the marriage ended. But what was utterly astounding to me was that a strange and unexpected peace settled in. Wait a minute! I was *supposed* to be feeling lousy! I knew how lousy I had felt upon being dumped in high school. I knew how lousy I had been feeling during my effort to reconcile. So why was I experiencing peace? There was only one rational explanation in my view: I brought God into the equation for the first time in my life, and he had seen to a different emotional outcome. I placed all my eggs into the "God-obedience" basket and did everything I could to restore the marriage, because that was what I believed God wanted me to do.

Throughout that miserable period, I had a strong sense that God was watching my conduct closely. I even recall telling people who were wondering if I was sane for hanging on for so long that *I wanted to be able to look God in the eye and say I had left no stone unturned* in my attempt to resuscitate my marriage. At one point during my efforts, I even embarrassed my kind mother-in-law in one phone call with breaking down and blubbering over my inability to get her daughter back. She likely had not experienced too many grown men crying on the phone. Me either.

So after all this nuclear emotion, this incomprehensible peace reigned. I was feeling no pain! No stomach ache, no misery index, no mourning, no nothing. It was wild. I remember being at dinner with friends, an accountant and his wife, and telling them about this phenomenon in my life. What's more, I rather boldly told them I believed it was God honoring my obedient effort to restore my marriage by now giving me great peace. You should have seen the looks on their faces. I could absolutely read their thoughts, *Oh, dear—our friend Wes has completely lost his mind.* They weren't exactly religious types. The wife was a counselor at some facility who likely saw crazy people every day and figured she recognized one across the dinner table from her. She responded to my declaration with just a hint of a pathetic "oh, please" twist: "Oh, Wes, don't you think you are just repressing?"

I had pretty much blown off psychology class in college, so I wasn't sure I knew what "repressing" meant. But I could catch the drift from the faint, albeit loving, sneer. Doubtless she figured I was in so much pain that I was in a kind of pathetic shock and was stuffing my emotions. If I could only get a hold of my inner child I would come to realize just how very miserable I really and truly was.

But next came the pivotal moment: I looked her in the eye and the following fell out of my mouth, "I guess I will know this was God and not my repressing if I can ever imagine my ex-wife being physically with another man and it not hurting!" The ultimate test.

It was a few weeks later and my Sunday school singles class was going out to a movie. Not just any movie but a movie *event*. One of the women in the class was a radio DJ and she had free tickets to a sneak preview movie that had been promoted on her station. So a bunch of the class showed up at the Quail Springs theaters on a Thursday night. The place was absolutely packed out, standing room only. We got there early enough to grab seats on the middle right as one walks into the theater. We were all cutting up and having a good time in the dull light of the auditorium. Our attention was unavoidably drawn to a couple kissing across the aisle and down a few rows. We snickered. It was pretty distracting—we were a singles class after all! We were mesmerized. Yet, as my eyes became increasingly adjusted to the poor lighting, the back of the woman's head began to slowly take shape into a familiar form. Suddenly, I found my head poking forward like a turtle on alert and I had to almost grab my plunging jaw as I realized who it was. My wife! Or rather, my ex-wife! I was absolutely stunned! I couldn't believe it. Right there, not twenty feet away, I was being confronted by my ex-wife in the arms of another man.

And I felt absolutely *nothing*. No stomach ache, no anger, no misery index. Other than my initial shock, there was simply *nothing*. I merely watched the movie. I think Kurt Russell was in it. It was really pretty good.

After the movie was over I walked alone out to my truck, opened the door and plopped behind the wheel. Reflecting on what I had observed with my ex-wife, I actually said out loud, *Gee, Lord, why would you want me to see that?* There was an immediate response. It was not an audible voice, but it was like this instantaneous burst inside my head. It was a statement, out of the blue, a responsive comment the likes of which I had not even considered. It was the still, small voice of God belting it out like he had been poised, eager, and waiting for me to pop that question behind the wheel.

You set the question! The Voice said.

Naturally, I was taken aback. I had completely forgotten about what I said to the couple at dinner a few weeks earlier. Suddenly it was clear. What were the odds of running into her at all, much less seeing what I saw on a Thursday night in a packed out theater and me with a front row seat to boot? The whole scene had been divinely orchestrated, and if that had not become clear on my own, God actually answered my mumbled query. He wanted me to know I was right, that it *had* been him who brought peace in the face of despair. He *is* real! He *is* involved! He *cares* about *me*! My suspicion of his kindness in the aftermath of divorce turned to conviction. By demonstrating the payoff to obedience, my "Personal Trainer" had just helped build up the muscle of my faith and knocked a large chunk off of my monument to Skepticism. It would not be the last time.

Recovering from Cool

God might have spoken to me in that parking lot, but I still had to go back to my dumpy apartment. I was still in financial ruin. It was still the worst time of my life. There were mornings I would literally let my fingers do the walking through the pages of scripture seeking verses on "patience" or "trust" or "peace." It was as if I was in some sort of spiritual rehab, detoxing off the ego binge of thinking I was so cool. Of course, I had never been spiritual, so there wasn't much to rehabilitate.

I was being forced to transfer my love affair from myself to my God. I was terribly lonely and by the world's standard I was a miserable failure. I was twenty-nine years old, divorced and heavily in debt. I once thought I was going to be rich by then, or at least very, very important. A real somebody. I spent the next two years with a failing business but a growing relationship with God. I had a lot of help from good men with the latter. Besides singles class I also attended a Thursday morning Bible study at church. All the men there were old enough to be my father and they really took me under their wing. Guys like our pastor, David Cotten, Ralph Mason, Ralph Jenks, Bill Boulton, Jack Wentz, Bill Svejkovsky and Hank Warren, to name a few. These guys gathered around me, wise men of God, taking me through the paces of walking the walk and not just talking the talk. I will always be deeply, deeply grateful to them.

Even though I was desperately trying to be obedient, I still treated God like an embarrassing relative at times. I was mortified when, on my thirtieth birthday, John Dwyer came to my surprise party and there, in front of all my rather "secular" friends, plopped onto the table in front of everyone an unwrapped book titled *Loving God,* by Chuck Colson. I was apoplectic that my friends would see me receive a *Christian* book with such a sissy title as though I might actually read it. It was weeks before I got bored enough one night to actually do so. I was struck by just how profoundly Colson's book spoke into my life of that moment as it reflected on men and women throughout history who expressed their love of God through their obedience. This was the lesson I was learning and the chiseling tool God used on my skepticism. The more I loved Christ by my obedience, the more he was showing up in my circumstances. There was a significant quote Colson used in the book by a famous German pastor and theologian who had been martyred for his faith by the Nazis during World War II:

Only he who believes is obedient; only he who is obedient believes.
—Dietrich Bonhoeffer

In our walk with God, I know there have to be times when he jumps in and helps, sometimes without us even realizing it. Like circumventing a car wreck or something similar. He doesn't feel the need to announce his involvement every time he intercedes in our lives. Not every instance is an overt "God Moment" of the sort I had at the movie theater. Then there are times the Master sort of leaves smudges from his fingerprints, leaving us a strong suspicion he is invading our lives once again. He is kind like that. I was also learning that God takes advantage of our situations to make points and give tests. One of my many challenges was the fact that I was very lonely and very much a healthy male. I actually had to occasionally meet with John Dwyer just for him to throw spiritual ice water on me to cool me off. Fortunately, God provides us support throughout our travels with Him. John was one of those critical supports during a key season. Especially with helping me stay out of trouble with women. Of course, I didn't tell him about Sally.[3]

Smelling the Holy Rat

Sally (not her real name) worked at the University of Oklahoma and was very cute besides having a tremendous personality. My business caused our interaction and, since it was all business of course (of course!), I asked her to lunch. We hit it right off. By then my dad had become a Christian and observed that one of the neat things about getting with other Christians was that once one person brings up Jesus in the conversation, the other cannot resist jumping on the subject like the proverbial hungry duck after a June bug. Like two sports enthusiasts talking about their favorite team, Christians find Jesus an exciting subject and cannot resist discussing him. So, my dad's thought went, I could sort of measure someone's spiritual interest in Jesus with a subtle mention of the Lord and see if the listener would "jump" on it and want to discuss spiritual things. Truth be told, I was also afraid (okay, paranoid) of getting involved with a female without similar spiritual interests. I knew that it was my relationship with God that had compelled me to hang in with my marriage to the end and, if I were to get married again, I wanted that partner to hang in there with me out of their relationship with God rather than fall prey to whatever circumstances might be making life inconvenient. In short, I was terrified of being dumped again.

At lunch I somehow adeptly managed to toss out a "Jesus" June bug comment to see if Sally would hop on it. She didn't seem to take the bait. It was actually a pretty lame response. But hey, limp wasn't exactly like there had been *no* response at all! I rationalized it all the way. Maybe she just hadn't understood.

This is one of those "fingerprint smudges" that after many years of experience I *strongly* suspect God worked as an intervener, kindly jumping in to save me from myself. After that lunch, I called Sally up to ask her out. She couldn't that night but counter-offered "how about such-and-such a night?" Ah, she was interested. Well, I couldn't do it that night. We agreed to try another time. Over the next few weeks (and I'm a little embarrassed to admit this), I asked her out *thirteen* times. No joke. I was counting and each time I picked up the phone to call her I became a little more like the drug addict trying desperately to meet with his drug dealer. I couldn't believe I could not get a date fix! This had never happened to me in my entire life! What made it worse and kept luring me to make those calls was that I could tell she actually *wanted* to go out with me. A blind man could see that. Alas, we could *never* make that date happen. I think she finally lost interest and for all I know even developed a boyfriend relationship with someone who was a better scheduler. All I lost was a bit more pride, yet something was clearly thwarting this thing from the beginning.

That's when I smelled the Holy Rat (no disrespect intended). Deep in my heart I knew God knew that *I even knew* that Sally was not right for me. But I had weakened. It was at that moment I came to the crashing understanding that the Lord would not allow me to meet the right girl until I was content with just him and me, together and alone. I needed to be his "date" for awhile before I could handle being someone else's. I needed too much work.

I suspect some of you are thinking this is pretty lame. No voices, no lightning, no audacious miracles and *I think God did something*? (Just now I'm feeling like the guy who claims he saw bigfoot but the camera was out of film.) But God is the perfect Father. Have you ever hovered over your little child, or maybe even your favorite pet, and just caught yourself smiling from the pure pleasure of your love? Have you ever just reached out and maybe moved aside an object to keep your child from stumbling and they didn't even notice you did that? The object was there one second and the next it was gone because you could see the big picture and your child wasn't strong enough to handle it. The Bible says we are made in our Maker's image. When we do something like that, that is the Creator's imprint upon our being. God hovers over me because he crazy loves me. He loves all of his children. Sometimes he lets us hit the wall of our conduct, and sometimes he just moves it out of our way.

"Dad" Finally Figures I'm Ready

It was around two lonely years later before I met Lori on a blind date. Indeed, I had finally become content with just me and God. Even though I was always on the lookout for a prospective mate, I was not like a careening fool any longer.

Butch McCain, one-half of the popular local morning television news team of the time with his brother, Ben, gave me a call to tell me about this beautiful doctor he wanted me to meet. At the time he was dating (and is now married to) Lori's sister, Betty, whom I had met a year or so earlier. I confess I was still paranoid about the dating scene. I was trying hard to take my relationship with God very seriously and I was acutely aware and infinitely nervous about falling for someone not on the same spiritual page. Poor Lori. I only reluctantly agreed to go to lunch with her, because I must sheepishly confess that in my youthful ignorance I still doubted seriously that there could possibly be any cute girls actually graduating from medical school, much less a practicing facial plastic surgeon. I know what you are thinking, and you are right. Here I was, all consumed with this self-holier-than-thou business and yet still afflicted with the attitude of "please God, let her be a babe." It appears I was still a work in progress. Or, as Lori might say, I was simply a dumb boy.

I arrived at her office to pick her up and was distracted by a beautiful woman in a red dress in the reception area. *Wow!* I thought, *what a great looking receptionist!* She introduced herself, and then I tried picking my jaw up off the floor. It was Lori! Still, my paranoia quickly reclaimed the moment and I steeled myself to not fall for a pagan in my lonely and vulnerable state. Lori and I today have a running dispute concerning that lunch. She insists I was putty in her hands and that I,

like all men, was more than willing to talk about myself for the entire
lunch duration. She claims she merely plied me with questions and I
was content to talk about the fascinating subject of me. I dispute that,
of course. I cannot speak for other men.

Lori shared with me over lunch that she was born and raised on a
Kansas wheat farm (clear evidence right there, Lori, that the lunch
conversation was not all about me!). It was a remarkable story and after
I took her back to her office, we went through some photos on her
office wall. We came to one of her and a famous Beverly Hills facial
plastic surgeon, Frank Kamer, in an operating room accompanied by
a note to "the best fellow I ever trained"—Lori. She had done a one
year fellowship with this "surgeon to the stars" who would later want
her to be his partner. I looked at that photo and looked at her and said,
"How does a Kansas farm girl end up working with a famous Beverly
Hills plastic surgeon?" To which she responded with the sentence that
changed the course of my life: "Oh, it was the Lord!"

I thought the Hallelujah Chorus was going to break out all over
again! The earth moved, the angels sang, a lightning bolt shot forth
from the finger of God! This was a beautiful, engaging, intelligent,
gen-u-ine Christian female!

We were married six months later.

Well, that is not fair. Actually, it wasn't all that easy. I did have to
convince her that marrying me was a good idea. After all, from the
world's point of view I would have been easily considered a Loser with
a capital L. All I owned was a humongous business debt and a basset
hound named Andrew.

In the interest of being fair, Lori was a bit paranoid of me as well. We
ended up having a number of cross examination sessions (she might say
"inquisitions") in which I would artfully and sensitively probe into her
belief systems to more fully understand her heart. She would say that I
was just trying to get her to say what I wanted her to say. She can be a
bit stubborn. We can both easily agree that our dating life was far more
arduous than our married life has ever been (I know it is supposed to be
the other way around). Plus, after my first marital debacle, I had read
every book there was on being the "sensitive" male, been to Christian
counseling galore, blah, blah, blah. I wasn't going to see my ship sunk

this time. It was Lori's first marriage and it was going to be my last. I have learned that involves a certain degree of understanding those very key words "Yes, ma'am" and "I'm sorry" and "Darling, what do *you* think we should do?"

But what was amazing to me was that Dr. Lori Hansen looked past my baggage and my loser status. Someone told us that in determining whether we should marry, we should ask the question "will we glorify God more as a couple than we will as individuals?" Looking back, I still don't know how she knew the answer to that one. We were married September 11, 1987. My years with her have been the best of my life.[4]

This "wilderness period," as I have referred to my years away from the DA's office, were drawing to a close and would officially end when I returned to the Oklahoma County District Attorney's office on September 15. I scoffed at ever returning to that line of work, despite many encouraging me to do so. I thought it was over. Yet, running around my high school track one evening before Lori and I were married, the thought traversed my mind like a shooting star, and it was actually accompanied by something like a sweet taste in my mouth. I was shocked that it was a pleasant thought. I know now how the Holy Spirit works. Shortly after that I called Mr. Macy and had lunch with him. I didn't say I wanted a job, because I was still very tentative in my thoughts. I just felt drawn to be around my old boss and get his advice on life in general. He was very gracious. I'm sure he saw right through me and knew I was thinking of resuming my prosecutorial career. Not long after that I got a call from his first assistant Pat Morgan offering me my old job back. I was honestly surprised by the racing of my heart. To top it off, I would actually have a regular paycheck again, after digging my financial hole. I called up Lori and asked her what she thought I should do. I submit this as Exhibit A that I really had learned something about relationships during my wilderness period. Very sweetly she said, "Well, I think you should first think about it and then call back and say *Yes*." For once, I did what I was told. It was a God thing.

CHAPTER THREE

WHO YOU GONNA BELIEVE?
ME, OR YOUR LYIN' EYES?

Murder is the sad circumstance in which through no fault of their own, someone's fifteen minutes of fame comes over their own dead body. All our lives we yearn to be remembered, to be known, to believe our existence matters. All of which is why becoming a celebrity in death is such a dark thing. The beauty of a life finding itself overshadowed by the ugly notoriety of whatever evil last touched it. For all of that which was Susan Hamilton's full and vibrant life, her celebrity came only by way of her grisly death and now the murder trial of her accused husband, John, was grinding slowly to a conclusion.

It was December of 2001, and although the judge and courtroom décor had not changed since the previous March's bond hearing, things had certainly changed for me. I was by that time the District Attorney for Oklahoma County, having been so appointed by the governor the previous summer. Coming into office in the midst of media frenzy over Oklahoma City bombing co-conspirator Terry Nichols' prospective state trial, the media attention surrounding the Hamilton case was itself quite significant. Before it was all said and done the Valentine's Day tragedy would draw national attention.[1] But the trial also came right in the middle of Lori and my own personal trials as it had only been the previous month that her struggles with a prescription drug addiction had become very public. In public, I sought to maintain the

33

requisite steady persona of the chief prosecutor doing justice without distraction even while my own wife was being savaged in the press. How does one maintain equilibrium during that after all? Put lightly, it was not without its challenges. One particular night, not long before the Hamilton trial began, but in the midst of all the media tumult with which we were as a couple contending, I found myself turning to Lori in the quiet darkness of our bedroom and exhaling the thought that had just crossed my mind. "I do not know how anyone goes through these sorts of things without God . . . to what do they tether themselves?" It wasn't meant to be a cheap platitude offered to a discouraged wife. It was simply an observation that would prove increasingly prophetic as our tenure in the public eye raucously sallied forth. So when the wind of adversity becomes a hurricane, to what does one secure oneself? I had actually wondered that many times in dealing with victims of violent crime—real people struggling through catastrophic suffering. Lori and my personal public struggle was deep and painful but nothing in comparison to what Susan Hamilton's children and family were experiencing.

The courtroom was yet again packed. Hamilton's skeptical supporters were back in force but this time joined by an array of the media and the simply curious. The back benches of jury trials are often thinly populated by folks that find public spectacle far more entertaining than television soaps. As for me, this time I was not alone, having acquired the help of a very able assistant prosecutor as well as a pair of homicide detectives from the Oklahoma City Police Department who, amongst others, had done a great deal of very fine police work investigating the case.[2]

The evidence against Hamilton was simply overwhelming. Despite failed behind-the-scenes attempts on the part of his lawyers to get the judge to allow them to muddy the water by introducing speculation that she might have been murdered by mysterious abortion protesters, there was nothing the jury was hearing or seeing that could point to any *reasonable* explanation of her murder other than his having been the culprit. Hamilton himself had taken the stand in an effort to explain away the pile of evidence stacked against him. His explanations were often bizarre and nonsensical. An example of these exchanges surrounded a part of the deadly assault on Susan, which consisted of her being strangled with a pair of his neckties. Having thick and well-defined fingernails, deep and dramatic nail imprints were present on her neck where she had torn at her own flesh in a desperate bid to obtain relief from being choked. Fresh, seeping, and similar wounds were observed and photographed on John Hamilton's upper right arm and shoulder. Wounds consistent with her having put up a brief fight before being overwhelmed, wounds that I questioned him concerning after having displayed comparative photographs of the twin sets of wounds for the jury.

> **Lane**: Do you think it's kind of a shocking coincidence that the medical examiner would testify that the size of the wound on your upper shoulder there or back upper right arm would be consistent with what he would expect to see if that were a fingernail mark?
>
> **Hamilton**: I think that that kind of mark could be made by lots of things. And I can't—
>
> **Lane**: Paper clip?
>
> **Hamilton**: Oh, I think I would be a little more realistic than that.
>
> **Lane**: But it's an unfortunate coincidence, is it not, sir?
>
> **Hamilton**: It is not uncommon for me to have scratches.
>
> **Lane**: That look like fingernails?
>
> **Hamilton**: It doesn't look like fingernails to me.
>
> **Lane**: It doesn't?
>
> **Hamilton**: No.
>
> **Lane**: Although it did to the medical examiner and to the police.
>
> **Hamilton**: I think it depends on your—if you had seen those scratches in a different circumstance you probably wouldn't have thought that.
>
> **Lane**: All right.

I moved on to other topics. I had learned over the years that if someone was going to insist that a cat was a dog on the witness stand, it was best to just take pains to make sure the jury heard it with their own ears and then simply change the subject. We touched on a number of other matters during the course of a long cross examination, several of which drew similar raised eyebrow responses from the jury.

But the final nail in Dr. Hamilton's "innocence" coffin was to come from his own expert witness, one of the foremost authorities on blood stain pattern evidence in the country. To a significant degree the case always hinged on the issue of blood evidence. Where is it found and what does it tell us? Does it help identify the culprit? Did the fact that John Hamilton was drenched in blood in certain areas point to a man that got bloody trying to save his wife, or did it say something else? To say I was anxious about what this witness would say is an understatement. We had already presented our blood stain pattern expert and rested our case. We believed, for example, that particular tiny drops of blood (known as directional "spatter") on his shoes could only have come from the spray resultant from beating her with a blunt instrument and blood from that beating spraying onto his shoes—and not from his claim of becoming bloody for having given her CPR.

In the end, it wasn't the blood on his shoes that shocked the jury and the entire courtroom. It was the blood that my own expert had missed but that Hamilton's expert had not. I wish I could say that it was my withering cross examination that had forced a sweating and beaten expert to cough up the presence of those tiny drops inside his right shirt sleeve cuff. Instead, it was the honest answer to a simple question. I simply asked him if we had missed anything in our examination of the blood evidence that had not been presented to the jury. The answer, to the audible gasp from Hamilton's counsel table, was "yes."

Looking back, it was one of those Perry Mason once-in-a-lifetime career moments when everything goes into slow motion and the pounding of your heart in your ears almost drowns out the sound of your own voice. A cold sweat broke out on the back of my neck as I knew that whatever it was that we had missed could not be good for the defense. If it was something good for them, Hamilton's lawyer would have already brought it out in hopes of destroying my case. Instead, it was the expert's reputation for honesty and excellence in combination with the fact that my own pair of blood experts had assured me that there was nothing in the blood evidence that pointed to Hamilton being innocent that made it a question worth asking. I had him get off the witness stand and show the jury the tiny blood stains he indicated were inside Hamilton's shirt cuff. An entire courtroom virtually held its breath as he moved toward me and the bloody white dress shirt I held in my hand.

When one throws a rock into a pond there is a splash sending droplets of water into different directions. It is the same when a blunt instrument breaks open the human skull. Tiny blood drops or "spatter" go places in such a way that an experienced eye can determine from what direction the blood originated. There had already been such a blood soaking on Hamilton's shirt sleeve that a couple of key, very minute droplets were not observed, tiny streaks of blood that left a pattern on the shirt. As the defense expert explained, what had driven that blood up and into the shirt sleeve with its tell-tale pattern was most probably only one thing, and that was that the wearer of that shirt had struck the head of Susan Hamilton with a blunt instrument causing blood to be sprayed into his shirt cuff interior. Whoever wore that shirt had murdered Susan Hamilton—and the man arrested wearing that shirt was her husband, John Hamilton. The jury took less than two hours to convict him of murdering his beautiful wife on Valentine's Day morning.

Yet throughout the entirety of the trial with the collective weight of layer upon layer of evidence permanently closing the door on John Hamilton's freedom, even with the damning testimony of his own expert, there were still the skeptical few. The truly hardcore. The initial thronging mass of largely female supporters having melted away with the presentation of trial evidence. With this small group it would probably not have mattered had there been a video tape of Susan's violent death with her husband center frame. They were invested in their position on behalf of John Hamilton and were determined to cling to it. For Hamilton's hardcore supporters the evidence meant nothing. It reminded me of the old tale of the husband who had been caught by his wife in bed with another woman. "You're having an affair!" she screams. "That is not true," he defiantly claims, leaping up to throw on some clothes. "Of course it's true!" she exclaims. The husband points an accusing finger at her and declares, "Who are you gonna believe? Me, or your lyin' eyes?"

For whatever psychological reason, Hamilton's few remaining supporters found it easier to believe it was their eyes that were lying to them. They would never believe the truth, regardless of the facts. It became apparent to me that clinging to their position of skepticism had become far and away more important than the truth itself.

I may never understand the *why* of that. I do know that when it comes to the question of God, many of us cling to a particular position because it has become an old friend and we are most comfortable in its company.

Even when the evidence to the contrary is convicting.

Our battle with skepticism never really ends. I know mine has not. It just manifests itself differently than it once did. Once it was about God himself, but now this continuing process is more about my ongoing struggle to believe God for ever greater things in the face of ever greater adversity and storms of doubt. The absence of experiencing God drove my skepticism initially, and not being open to or expecting such an experience compounded the matter. It was my change of heart on the subject that removed the wall I placed between God and me. Everything slowly began to change when I made a decision of the heart to walk a different path. I felt no emotional connection other than all my other options already exhibited utter failure. When I made the choice to be obedient to a God with whom I was familiar only intellectually, that same God met me and began feeding me with experiences of him. What followed was that the more I experienced him, the more I wanted and the more he responded in increasingly amazing and supernatural ways. This is what God wants for all of us. This is what a real and loving God has done for men and women throughout history—not just in the pages of Scripture.

It is all a pursuit of the heart.

PART II
THE PURSUIT OF HEART

I have found David the son of Jesse, a man after My heart, who will do all My will.

—Acts 13:22

CHAPTER FOUR

THE PAYOFF OF PURSUIT

Heart is about becoming moved by the things that move God. It is about the syncing of our hearts with the heart of God.

It was the summer of 1996 when a twelve year old girl named Crystal Dittmeyer went missing. She had been living in a south Oklahoma City apartment with her mother, Tammy, her six-foot-five-inch, three hundred pound step-father, Ben Crider, and her two little brothers. When her mother looked about the apartment searching for clues to her disappearance, all she found was a small pool of roughly one cup of blood in the master bedroom which DNA testing later established as belonging to Crystal. Nothing else was missing, not even a stitch of clothing. It appeared as though she had taken a shower in the bathroom that her mother shared with her step-father and then somehow, some-way bled out a cup of blood beside their bed as though she lay there without moving for a time. There were no explanatory blood trails or smears of blood found elsewhere that police would have expected an injured and bleeding twelve year old to have left. There was no sign of a struggle. It was as though Crystal had simply evaporated.

I first became involved with the case investigation shortly after its inception. I was serving as the director of the juvenile division for the district attorney's office. As such, I was initially contacted by Oklahoma

City Police detectives wanting to take Crystal's little brothers into protective custody as both mother and step-father were immediate suspects. This would require action at juvenile court, and the more I learned, the more I began assisting the investigation. I would end up remaining with the case. Crystal's body was never found.

To our knowledge, there had only been one other "body-less" murder case ever filed in Oklahoma County history[1] and that case had a whale of a lot more evidence than we did. Such cases are very rarely filed. The reason is simple. In order to charge a person with murder, one must first prove someone else is dead. Juries are not going to send someone to prison for life without being confident there really is a victim. For at least a couple of years detectives Bob Bemo, Bill Cook, and a number of others worked tirelessly on the case. We were convinced that the killer was Ben Crider, Crystal's step-father. We had caught him lying on various matters and very importantly, we had determined his garment bag to be missing. A search warrant on the apartment turned up evidence that he had purchased a brand new, identical bag shortly after Crystal's disappearance.

In a juvenile court hearing concerning Crystal's brothers, I managed to get Crider under oath admitting to purchasing the new bag but giving the wild tale that he had thrown away his original bag to prevent the police from "framing" him with it. He claimed he had tossed the missing bag in a dumpster. It was our theory that Crider needed to replace the bag because he had used it to wrap up her body and get her out of the apartment without leaving any other trace of blood.

It was a high profile case of the first order. Crystal's photograph was plastered all over the city on posters seeking her whereabouts. It was in the media a great deal. There were even "Crystal sightings," individuals who were convinced they had seen her somewhere since her disappearance. One person claimed to have spoken with her at Frontier City, a local amusement park, while another said she saw her at a local department store in a checkout line. One girl, a neighbor, claimed to have seen her that very afternoon and that Crystal told her she was running away. But for one reason or another, although these sightings were usually well meaning, we knew they were not credible. Still, it made the case very difficult to prove beyond a reasonable doubt, which to some juror minds means beyond *any* doubt at all (which it does not mean). The case was a massive jigsaw puzzle with teeny-tiny pieces. There was absolutely no proverbial "smoking gun," either proving she was dead or that her step-father committed the crime. A cup of blood was not a fatal quantity. We even held out hope that if we waited long enough before filing a charge, perhaps a hunter might stumble across her body out in a field or forest somewhere. It had happened before; it would not happen for us in this case.

Mr. Macy and his First Assistant District Attorney, Patrick Morgan, made it very clear that if I wanted to see this case filed then I had better plan on trying it personally. I wish I could claim it was because of my incredible trial skills, but truth be-known, it was because almost no other prosecutor wanted to touch it with a ten foot pole. I remember Mr. Macy's eyes boring down into me as he asked me if I could win this case. It wasn't the strongest "Yes" I'd ever given my boss, but I *knew* trying the case was the right thing to do, I *knew* Ben Crider was guilty, and I *knew* Crystal was dead. I told him the case wasn't going to get any better. To both their credit, these men ultimately trusted my judgment and that of the police. Had it been a question of only trying sure winners, as some prosecutors around the country are prone to do, it would have never left a police unsolved file. I filed the case in 1998.

It was one thing to file a murder charge and quite another to get a jury to hold Ben Crider responsible for Crystal's death. Fellow Assistant District Attorney, Richard Wintory, agreed to try the case with me. An outstanding trial attorney, Richard owed me big-time after I was his assistant trial counsel in another notorious murder case back in 1994, *State vs. Jimmy Ray Slaughter*. A diabolical killer, Slaughter tortured and murdered his girlfriend and then slew *their* baby using a craftily planned alibi. It was extraordinarily complex. Richard said it might take as long as six weeks to try. I caved in to my friend's earnest plea for help, thinking I would still easily be able to make the trip to Australia and New Zealand accompanying Lori, as she had been invited to teach at some medical meetings. It took over five long and arduous *months* to try the case. I missed the trip, but more importantly, the jury convicted a vicious murderer. Years later he was executed for his horrendous acts. Consequently, I figured Richard owed me a few weeks of his time.

Up to that point in time, I had rarely in my life felt the kind of pressure I felt during the Crider case. The stress was terribly reminiscent of a previous decade, finding myself separated from my first wife, drowning in debt, with creditors at the door. The detectives and I believed deeply, however, in the "righteousness" of this case (no religious reference intended). But during the summer of 1999, motion hearing after motion hearing began to slowly chip away piece after piece of our evidence as defense motions were sustained right and left. Our already difficult-to-prove case was leaking strength—and hope—like a torpedoed tugboat. It was this pressure that first drove me to read the psalms of David.

A Glimpse of "Heart"

Although I consistently read the Bible, to me the Psalms were something someone read when having difficulty sleeping. I thought them boring and of little current value. They ranked right up there with the mind numbing details associated with the institution of the tabernacle found in the book of Exodus. David was my hero, however, a favorite of God, and I so very much wanted to emulate his faithful walk and be such a man as he. It had been ten years earlier, in 1989, while sitting in our living room that I asked God to do just that—make me a man after his own heart like David. I believed then that I was a man lacking compassion. David was a man of deep compassion, and I wanted that. One of the many wonderful things I have observed about the Father is that he wants to accommodate us when we dare ask for attributes that please and honor him. I suppose I should insert a warning here. If we are serious about the acquisition of character traits that please God, he has a grand tendency to then chart character training programs that bear a remarkable resemblance to boot camps. We are proud once we graduate, but in the middle of the program we're wondering why we volunteered.

Out of anxiety and desperation in the Crider case I turned to David's psalms seeking peace. To be sure, I found peace, although since God is reading this I guess I had better be careful about sounding too holy on that one. Achieving "peace" was often like trying to hang on to a greased pig. But the unexpected treasure was discovering one of the key ways men and women after God's heart engage in prayer. It was not prayer like I was used to, and had it not been in the Bible, I would have wondered if it was "legal" in American Christianity. David's prayers were often *declaratory* and tough, not like the typical prayers of petition to which I was better accustomed—prayers which were more genteel and civilized. Not so "in your face." David's form of prayer seemed like it might make God mad or something. It even seemed arrogant. The more I drank them in, however, the clearer they became. They were neither arrogant nor designed to make God mad. Rather, they were designed to *initiate God's response.* These words plumbed the depths of a warrior's heart, a man unafraid of dying but terrified at the thought of going into battle without his King. A son who so clearly understood and was so very comfortable being around his heavenly Father that he didn't mind marching into the throne room and jerking violently on his Father's robes to get his attention.

David grasped the heart of God. He was moved by the things that moved God. God loved justice, and so did David. God hated evil, and David hated it as well. I don't wish to grossly oversimplify things, but their relationship itself was the sweet simplicity of the unabashed love between a small child and his doting father. David's prayers were brimming with the confidence of a son that completely expected his Father to respond to evil. David lived by an uncomplicated code: "Despise evil, love justice." Why? Because God did. It was his expression in Psalm 5 that became my "theme" psalm for the trial.

> Give ear to my words, O Lord, consider my meditation. Give heed to the voice of my cry, My King and my God, for to You I will pray. My voice you shall hear in the morning, O Lord; in the morning I will direct it to You and I will look up. For you are not a God who takes pleasure in wickedness, nor shall evil dwell with You. The boastful shall not stand in your sight; You hate all workers of iniquity, You shall destroy those who speak falsehood; the Lord abhors the bloodthirsty and deceitful man . . . For You, O Lord, will bless the righteous; with favor You will surround him as with a shield.
> —Psalm 5:1–6, 12

45

I was profoundly moved by David's directness with God. This was no manly "strong silent type" attitude. David was vocal and transparent to the greatest extent possible. If it was on his heart, it was on his lips to God. Many of us are reluctant to engage in prayer, and this is especially true for men. Prayer seems so mysterious and maybe even kind of weird. After all—didn't Jimmy Stewart talk to an invisible rabbit named "Harvey" in some old movie? Wasn't his character thought to be crazy?

Even the very word "prayer" seems less than manly. There is no contact sport associated with it. Can you imagine listening to sports talk radio and someone suddenly talking about "praying" for his favorite quarterback? Talk about injecting a chill into a hot topic. This might be different if we came up with other words to substitute for the word prayer, words that connote action, battle and victory. A word like, say, *blitzkrieg*. "I had a great time of blitzkrieg this morning!" "I'm blitzkrieging that my team will win the playoffs!" "I'm blitzkrieging for my family!" Hmmm. Anyway, many regard prayer as a sort of weakness at best, or waste of time at worst. What is the point? As a kid I was always told "God helps those who help themselves," although as yet I have been unable to find biblical backup for that concept.

This dim view of prayer certainly was *not* David's. He believed the victor in battle depended entirely on God's support. David, a *manly* man, a *dangerous* man, did not hesitate to bare his fears, hopes, and dreams before his God. He did not hesitate to call evil out and declare war on it on behalf of a justice-loving God. He expected to see God's response, and he did. David knew prayer was conferencing with the King of the universe; it was all about muscle and strength and power. As a man of action, he *did not take action* unless he had conferred with the one Individual who decided outcomes and had the ability to give his plans thumbs up or thumbs down. David knew then, just as we know now, that the world revolved around relationships and that we cultivate the relationships that matter. God mattered. That's prayer.

Warrior-Speak

Graham Cooke is a Christian author and speaker. He made an interesting observation in a presentation titled "Way of the Warrior."[2]

He pointed out that while we are all called to be soldiers in the service of God, not everyone is a "warrior." Whereas soldiers make petition in their prayers (i.e., making requests for things), warriors also make *declaration*. They react to circumstance by *declaring* God because they already recognize God's likely point of view on a matter. When I was a child, I could anticipate how my earthly father would react to certain matters because I hung out with him. *I knew him.* I could easily have responded to many situations with an emphatic "Dad wouldn't like that!" This was David's famous response when first observing Goliath and hearing the trash the giant was talking: "For who is this uncircumcised Philistine that he should taunt the armies of the living God?" (1 Sam. 17:26). David was offended on behalf of God, understanding God well enough even at his young age that he actually *declared* God's thoughts on the matter and acted in conformity with that knowledge. One could almost hear God giving a whoop and saying, "That's my boy!" The rest of the encounter made history.

David made war with his prayers. He saw life as warfare, whether with real swords or not. There would always be ongoing earthly warfare with evil. He also recognized that evil didn't always come dressed in a suit of armor, but that sometimes it came disguised in seemingly harmless ways, a cancer far more subtle than men with clubs. Such evil was no less offensive than the more overt variety. Evil was evil. Justice was justice. This man's man saw prayer as far more than just casual conversation; it was an instrument of combat.

Applying David

As I read those prayers of David, his psalms, I realized there *must* be something deeply relevant for God to so clearly receive prayers like David's—rough, emotionally violent, vicariously hurting over the things that bothered God. I realized that if David despised evil's assault on the innocent and he deigned it important to pray prayers of declaration, maybe I needed to re-examine my prayer life. If God despised murder, why be namby-pamby about it in my conferring with God about Crystal's murderer? Crystal Dittmeyer was an innocent child; her murder was evil. If the man after God's heart knew he needed to engage in warfare prayer, it must be the thing to do. As the trial approached, Lori and I began praying together as a couple for the first time on a nightly basis.[3] Up to that point our prayers had been separate issues. She did not know what was on my heart to bring before God, nor did I with her. (I don't recall what had catalyzed this new joint practice other than I asked her to do so.). Since 1998, I have kept a journal of my experience with God. Here is what I wrote concerning the first moment of divine intervention in the case, an intervention that came as a direct result of prayer. It would not be the last.

Journal: Wednesday, August 18, 1999

I cried out to the Lord this morning concerning the Crider case. It is set for trial on the 30th. The judge yesterday would not allow us a continuance to achieve the DNA testing we wanted. I found myself strangely calm in the face of that. Richard Wintory was just this side of furious. A part of me just wants to get this over with.

Bill Gothard gave me some materials concerning crying out to the Lord. The Lord's children throughout the Bible catalyst Him into action through their crying out. I have now done that and I will continue to do so. *I do not want to do this case under my own power.* I remembered David and his words concerning the twisted stories and deceptions spouted by those against him. I got on my face before the Lord, "Abba Father, Daddy!" The job of the defense is to confuse and confound. This case is entirely circumstantial; no body. I have nowhere to turn. I need my Father's Divine Intervention. I prayed Psalm 60 before him. I am clinging/fleeing to his banner of truth. I am asking that *he* lead this army; that he go forth and conquer; that this victory be *his* and no one else's. David chose to trust in the face of adversity and the enemy and his deceptions. I will do the same.

Journal: Thursday, August 19, 1999

Yesterday morning, Richard Wintory called concerning the DNA testing. It seems that, whereas we once thought it would take 3–5 months (!) to complete the tests, it can be done in 2 weeks! This is astounding really, and made us not just a little frustrated in that had we known that on Tuesday the judge might have passed the case for such a short period. But here is the interesting part. Richard immediately went to the judge to let her know about this. Before he could say a word, she gestured that he come back into her chambers. She expressed to him that she had been very restless the night before (Tuesday night), struggling over the decision she had made (I wish I had her exact words). She was so troubled that yesterday morning she called a Court of Criminal Appeals judge to seek his advice. The bottom line is that she changed her mind!! She was now willing to set the case over for as long as it took to finish the tests. Now that the testing can be done shortly, I think we are looking at September 13 for trial.

This is nothing short of astounding!

When I received this information, my first thought was, *"Had God done this in response to my prayers?"* I thought back to Tuesday night. After Lori and I had prayed, which had included prayer over this case, I felt compelled to lay prostrate before the Lord and continue to pray concerning the case. This was late in the evening, pushing 10 P.M. Then early the next morning I had particularly fervent prayer, having, as I said in that entry, reviewed some Davidic psalms. Is it coincidence that this judge would have been troubled throughout the evening and the next morning be moved to call a higher authority? Was her heart troubled because the Holy Spirit was moving upon her in light of my fervent prayer? Was any of this a result of my calmness in the face of adversity and telling the Lord that I would trust Him regardless of whether we had the DNA or not?????

Lori thinks this is a no-brainer. During our prayer time, as I was fumbling over myself during my prayer with him concerning these questions, Lori kind of interjected, asking the Lord to forgive me for my unbelief.

I was so excited to see God move that I became even more spiritually aggressive. Every day on the way to trial instead of doing what I had always done, which was to mentally review the case, I played praise and worship music. I wore out the Hillsongs CD "Shout to the Lord!" I knew that the God of the Bible was enthroned on the praises of his people.[4] Consequently, I decided that since I wasn't going to be able to do squat under my own feeble power, I was going to start acting like a man who actually believed the biblical rules of engaging in spiritual warfare. I'm sure there was more than one driver who thought I was a nut, singing at the top of my lungs as I drove down the Hefner Parkway to work. Also, at the request of a dear friend named Pat Ward, I put together a list of prayer requests for her to bring to a group of intercessors who would continually pray on behalf of our cause. The pressure was so very, very intense, but the Lord was teaching me a few things.

I had tried many cases throughout my prosecutorial career, and even then I had only lost a couple. Prior to Crider, I prayed milque-toast sorts of prayer before trials, but this was taking things to a whole new level. I began to remind God, as did David, of who he is and how he is a God of justice—in fact, that justice and righteousness are the very foundation of his throne.[5] I hammered away nightly, pleading my case before the Lord, always praying prayers of justice. I was particularly attracted to Psalm 17 in which David commences with "Hear a just cause, O Lord, attend to my cry," in which David actually saw himself as a just cause for God's attentions.

On one particular wrenching night prior to trial, Lori and I were in our bedroom; I lay on the floor intensely speaking out my feelings to God, the desperation so very deep. I cried out "Lord, if this is how you want me to pray, then find him guilty for he *is* guilty!" Lori interrupted me, thinking I had perhaps gone too far. "Don't you think we should ask Pastor Daub (an associate pastor in our church and dear friend) if it's okay to pray like that?" "No!" I responded. "This is how David prayed!"

It was shortly after that evening that something happened to change my life and cause me to be forever ruined for the ordinary. Lori was invited to a ladies prayer meeting by a friend. Now Lori, being the shy person she is, is not exactly prone to go to a meeting like that with a group of strangers (except for her friend). That decision in and of itself was surprising to me. Very importantly, Lori also did not share with these women what she and I had been praying concerning the trial. At some point in the evening, Dale, the lady leading the group and a perfect stranger to my wife, came up to Lori and said the following words: "The Lord would have you know that the matter about which you and your husband have been praying is a *just cause.*"

Now *absolutely no one* knew that Lori and I were fervently crying out to God that he would himself judge this case to be a "just cause!" For that matter, nobody even knew we were praying together period! Either Dale had a microphone in our bedroom, or Someone else was listening to our prayer sessions.

Lori came home and told me what happened. A supernatural God was listening to our prayers and he had graciously decided to send Wes and Lori Lane a message of encouragement through a complete and total stranger, someone totally ignorant of our circumstances. That had never happened to either of us in our entire lives. We certainly read about that sort of thing in the Bible, but for us this was a major head stretch. At least it was for me. Lori was not so challenged with the concept that God might actually be, well . . . God. Here I had been resolutely crying out for the Father, pleading for him to do justice in this case. Here I had obstinately refused to tone down the aggressive nature of my prayers. Here I ardently wanted to be a fellow after God's own heart like my hero David. Here God sent us a personal and supernatural message in response to our prayers. And . . .

I didn't want to believe it.

As I reflect back on my reaction, I cannot help imagining God, upon hearing my typical old "default" position of unbelief and skepticism, simply shaking his very patient head. What did I want—a burning bush? I can say from great experience, these "default" positions are tough to get rid of. Getting from a starter position of "Oh, c'mon now" to "I believe" has taken me years, and even now it rears its ugly head more than I care to admit. I'm just relieved I'm not the first child of God to be so challenged.

Many things happened during that case to bolster my faith as the Lord poured out his favor on us. Specific prayer after specific prayer was answered. From the amazing way we obtained an extraordinary jury during jury selection, to finding the witness who proved the defense's expert witness was a liar, to conclusively establishing that all the so-called "Crystal sightings" were simply and clearly wrong—and it went on and on. Like the once popular "transformer" toys of that era, the "torpedoed tugboat" we thought we were piloting transformed into something more akin to an aircraft carrier. We were in trial for a solid month. The jury shocked the courthouse by convicting Ben Crider of first degree murder. It would not be the last time I would see God intervene in response to believing prayer. It would not be the last time I was given what turned out to be a message from the Lord. It would also not be the last time I would learn something about spiritual warfare in the Crystal Dittmeyer case and how the war never really ends. These matters will have to wait for another chapter.

There is much more to the Christian life than meets the eye. It is a life's experience way beyond what I once thought even as a believer. It is a life worth pursuing. A life we will examine more closely in the next chapter. I wrote this in my journal when the Crider trial ended:

Journal: Sunday, November 7, 1999

We finished trial Friday afternoon, October 22nd. The jury came back about 3:30 P.M. with a verdict of guilty and gave him "Life." This has been one of the most phenomenal experiences of my lifetime for I learned how to speak with my heavenly Father; I learned how to be a "David." Sounds almost arrogant, doesn't it? But I say that with humility and amazement. I feel almost overwhelmed. . . .

CHAPTER FIVE

SPILLING THE BEANS

The words from our mouths reveal the hidden thoughts of our hearts. The more our words align with God's thoughts about us and our situation rather than our own limited perspective, the more we see God revealed in our circumstances.

As They Say, "Confession Is Good for the Soul"

Who may ascend into the hill of the Lord? Or who may stand in His holy place? He who has clean hands and a pure heart, who has not lifted up his soul to an idol, nor sworn deceitfully. He shall receive blessing from the Lord, and righteousness from the God of his salvation.

—Psalm 24:3–4

In the early 1990s, I was the chief prosecutor for a multi-jurisdictional drug task force. We operated out of a semi-secret location and were comprised of investigators from a variety of state and local agencies, a number of whom operated undercover. Occasionally, we would arrest people who were actually *relieved* to get caught—they were so tired of being on the run. They were often contrite and would tell us everything we wanted to know. They wouldn't play games and were ready to take their medicine. Invariably, we (the law) were much more inclined to want to help the repentant contrite person than the committed outlaws.

In one particular operation, we were wiretapping a biker gang organization that was smuggling methamphetamine from California. It came time to arrest everyone and to see who upon arrest would decide to "flip," in other words, change sides and become witnesses for us against their co-conspirators. They still went to prison for their deeds but their cooperation yielded a bit of mercy via a more lenient length of incarceration.

After investigating any group for months and becoming familiar with its membership and even the personalities of its members, it was always interesting to see who would "break" and who would not, and also what method of persuasion would be necessary to achieve their cooperation (no, we never got to use water-boarding). In a way, it was the "moment of truth" for these individuals; an opportunity to observe which of these criminals would have a change of "heart" and be ready to "get right." On this biker gang occasion, we had so many co-conspirators arrested that we actually had to take over some offices on the main floor of the district attorneys' office to have room to deal with them all at once. We needed a room for each person because we always isolated the arrested from one another in order for them not to get the chance to talk together and get their stories straight before we talked with them.

I walked into the sunny, small office in which my wary subject was seated, his hands handcuffed behind his back. The shock of his arrest was written all over limp body language and impassive face. At the first of the interrogation he was a hard head, unwilling to face the reality of all the evidence we had on him as I went down the list. After a while it became apparent that I was talking to a wall. I could see that a polite and gentlemanly interaction was not going to suffice—he just was not going to let us keep this painless. I changed tactics, dropped the gentleman stuff, and after a bit, my subject finally saw the light and agreed to cooperate. Needless to say, by the time I walked out of the office, a number of the secretarial staff eyes were wide as they could overhear my "chatting" through the wall. I still smile when I recall Larry Andrews' (the task force director) wry comment to someone about me as we made our way to the elevator: "You don't want to make the reverend mad."

There are a couple different kinds of confession. One is made out of the brokenness of the heart and the other is made because it is the only way to survive. My biker pal's confession was certainly the latter. It had nothing to do with him being broken hearted over his criminal conduct. It was all about saving his bacon. It was also very common for these guys to "minimize" in their "confessions." In other words, tell us part, but not all, of their criminal involvement. If they minimized, we knew they still wanted to be a bad guy. The point of arrest was always a watershed moment; the proverbial fork in the road. That moment of choice revealing whether the bad guy wanted to "go straight" or stay on the crooked path.

As Christians, we are really not so different in our walk with God. We have failings as well. We have our own watershed moments—points of decision and forks in the road. Sometimes we also choose to be hard-heads. Perhaps we choose to minimize our responsibility. We don't want to admit we were wrong. Sometimes, I suspect, we even end up ticking God off, forcing him to change tactics until the hot temperature of our circumstance is sufficient to achieve our cooperation. That probably doesn't earn us any points with him. Walking God's path is never easy, but it can be a lot harder than it already is when we fail to cooperate. It is all a matter of heart. God may allow us to reap our consequences, but the purity of our heart may well determine whether he is willing to extend mercy in the midst of our circumstance.

David understood what to do when he got "arrested" by God through Nathan over his adultery and murder in 2 Samuel chapter twelve. His immediate response was to repent and confess. He held nothing back and hoped for mercy. The penalty under the law for his conduct should have been death. Instead, God allowed David to choose from lesser punishments. What is important about the king is that he was not just trying to cut his losses. He had a genuinely contrite and repentant attitude. It was the purity of his *heart* that saved David's life and convinced God that he could remain a useful man.

Thank You, but My Grudge and I Are Old Friends

I love how the Bible depicts its heroes warts and all. And boy, are there plenty of warts. It doesn't try soft soaping people but rather strips naked their hearts in order that we might more readily see the Great Cardiologist do his transforming work. It has always been a comfort to me to witness this revelation and process. God is the most incredibly patient and forgiving Person I know.

When he was a teenager, I often wanted to throttle our son, Derrick. I strongly suspect he wanted to throttle me even more. Having been his age, I knew that deep in the airy recesses of that teenager mental goop called a "brain" he was probably sizing me up and fantasizing whether he could "take me." Yet, just as I was apprehensive with my own father concerning just how far I could push him without losing my life, I suspected that Derrick was also a wee bit worried. My philosophy on dealing with teenage misconduct was simple: "Do bad things and bad things *will* happen to you." I vividly recall my father telling me what he hoped would happen to me if I were put in jail. Essentially, I was not to bother calling him if I was found attractive by my cell mates. Derrick, realizing I was a prosecutor, probably suspected I had the jail on speed dial and was more than willing to reserve him a room. Yet even in those rare, difficult times when our relationship was strained because of his rebellion on some matter, all it took was the slightest remorse on his part to dissipate all the tension like a punctured balloon. Our relationship was restored, my love no longer frustrated, and when he would then ask me for my help on something, there was nothing I was more pleased to do. I so wanted to bless his life in every way I could possibly think of. I still do.

That parental experience is the image of God being reflected in our lives. When our child admits (confesses) his or her wrong doing and changes their attitude, we as parents are prepared to do back flips on their behalf because we so love them. They *shall* receive our blessing because their attitude is wonderful in our eyes.

God gave me a good lesson on the importance of my confessing the sin of unforgiveness a few years ago. It was May of 2004. I was in Washington D.C. attending a meeting of the National District

Attorney's Association of which I was a board member. I had just finished reading a wonderful little book by Gregory Frizzell entitled *How
to Develop a Powerful Prayer Life.*[1] It was an excellent book. Shortly
before this D.C. conference, I met Dr. Frizzell at a prayer gathering.
He worked for the Southern Baptist Convention of Oklahoma and
was kind enough to give me a copy of his book (I subsequently gave
away dozens of the books to men in my church, some of whom were
powerfully impacted). As I read the book in my hotel room that morning, I was struck by a critical point made by Frizzell—the importance
of confessing our sins before God in prayer. This must be done before
asking him for help on matters, because sin is a major impediment to
God's willingness to hear our prayer.[2] Again, this speaks to the subject
of having "clean hands and a pure heart" before God. Frizzell also
pointed out that if nothing came to mind that needed clearing up,
to just *ask* the Lord if there was something! To be honest, I had never
considered *asking* God if there was a problem. Frizzell also asked the
question, "Are you bitter or holding grudges against people who have
offended you?"[3] He quoted Jesus in Matthew chapter six concerning
our need to forgive if we expect forgiveness. As I sat there on the bed, I
honestly couldn't think of anyone I needed to forgive. But, just in case,
I rather sheepishly decided to follow Frizzell's advice and ask God if
there was anyone I needed to forgive. Was there ever.

I was amazed to experience that no sooner had I *asked* him to reveal
to me if there was anyone I needed to forgive, than the name *Steve F—*
popped into my head! *I had not thought of Steve in years* and immediately
upon his name popping into my head I could feel the animosity surge
within me. Steve had been one of my best friends in high school. He
attended another high school but we attended the same church and the
year or so we hung out together was a magical period of my youth. We
had a blast together. He was a year ahead of me and ultimately went off
to college. We kept something of a relationship going over the next few
years, albeit tentative. Yet when my first wife had left me and I reached
out to him for help he had been too busy. It hurt me beyond measure. I
had harbored a simmering anger with him for many years. I had buried
my feelings about him, however, at least until God answered my prayer
and the Holy Spirit brought him to mind.

To say the least, I wasn't exactly in the mood to forgive Steve. I had neither seen nor talked to him in over twenty years! This, I might add, was just dandy with me. Out of grudging obedience I hurled my grudging forgiveness of Steve up to the Lord and considered that I had done my duty. The jerk!

I flew home and the following Monday I appeared in my office. My secretary, Sheila Harder, handed me a stack of message slips and as she did so told me that a Steve F— had called me from California. What?! I was stupefied over the timing of his call. She went on to tell me that he was coming into town in a couple of weeks and wanted to get together with me! *Over my dead body*, I graciously thought. Hmmm, well, maybe I needed to do a little more work on this forgiveness thing. I no more wanted to see Steve than share a glass of water with a flu carrier. That night I struggled with the message slip. God in his typically supernatural fashion was sending me a message. As I said, this is a *super*-natural path he has for us. He was serious about this forgiveness business and I determined not to go stupid on the matter and think this just an amazing coincidence. God had indeed spoken to me in my hotel room! There was no other explanation.

I ended up getting on my knees (I don't always pray on my knees, but this one required some heavy duty focus). I struggled with it for awhile and would occasionally test my level of real forgiveness by imagining myself having to be with Steve in some setting. Finally, after awhile I could tell I had really forgiven him and the Lord was very gracious as I at last got to a point I could envision the joyfulness of our meeting.

To add to the supernatural nature of the experience, when I called Steve I learned from him that God had impressed upon his heart that he needed to reconnect with me! Now my mind was really getting blown. We were both responding to a command from God. When we got together with our wives later it was amazing. He had become a pastor in California. I had resolved not to share with him my hurt from years before as that would only establish that I hadn't really forgiven him and that I wanted to punch back by letting him know how much he had hurt me. Yet, at that restaurant as we were catching up over two decades I could tell this entire night was a "God meeting" and I finally shared the supernatural nature of our gathering, how God spoke to me in that hotel room, and that our getting together was an act of an active and loving God. Steve wept when I shared with him how God had orchestrated things on *both* ends. He had had no idea of the pain I felt over the years but we were ecstatically joyful over the supernatural wonder of it all. Our reconciliation had been twenty years in the making and the blessing of it was simply beyond expectation. Later he sent me the CD of the sermon he preached a couple of weeks later on our story. He called it "The Miracle of Reconciliation."

King David knew about the importance of having "clean hands and a pure heart." The way to have such a set of clean hands and a pure heart is, of course, to avoid doing wrong things. But if we do sin, then we have the opportunity to confess these things and get the load off of us. David knew God blesses us for doing that because our heavenly Father is the Ultimate Parent. Just as we would do so for our own children, how much more should we expect our Father will do just that for us as well? It is simply *who He is* and it was that humble heart of David's that just lit God's rockets. God blessed both me and Steve for our obedience by healing an old wound and restoring an old friendship. That was very kind. God loves us so very much in even the smallest detail.

Weenie vs. Warrior Prayer

I used to think it odd that in his psalms David would always use mandatory language when it came to what God would or would not do. He did not give God any wiggle room on matters. It was always God *shall* do this or *shall* do that. If it had been up to me, I would have cut God some slack declaring *God might do this or might do that,* giving him a cosmic loophole of sorts so I wouldn't feel too bad if he did not feel obliged to do whatever it was. Of course, my giving God the big "maybe" is not exactly a tremendously faith-filled prayer on my part. But the fact that David talked in mandatory terms demands real scrutiny considering God regarded him as a role model. After all, David was not "the idiot" after God's heart; he was "the man." We should presume that since David's declaratory comments are Scripture and since God had great regard, then there must be some connection between the way he talked about God and the legacy he now enjoys. David went about *declaring* the character of God because he understood it. Clearly, God appreciated that and we should pay attention.

As I stated earlier, Graham Cooke made that interesting remark discussing the difference between a Christian "soldier" and a Christian "warrior." Warriors are so confident in the consistency of God's character that they dare to declare him in the midst of their circumstance. They know their Father so very well that their declaration is essentially boasting *in him*. God loves that. Who wouldn't? Especially when one has the capacity to actually *do* what is being boasted! Whether Old Testament figures like David or New Testament apostles like Paul,[4] the best of the best *dared to declare* God's unchangeable majesty over matters concerning which he had already spoken his mind or expressed his character.

Perhaps the most famous example of this was when David declared of Goliath, "Who is this uncircumcised Philistine that he should defy the armies of the living God?"[5] David's very comment reflects his clear comprehension of Israel's special relationship with God. Doubtless, every man in that army understood that intellectually. I suspect the story of Moses and the exodus from Egypt was hammered into the head of every Israelite child, as well as every other miracle of God recorded in the Pentateuch.[6] Just using common sense one can conclude that there was some percentage of that army that also sincerely believed what they were taught, and some were likely petitioning God to save them from Goliath! "Oh, God, please save us from Goliath and the Philistines!" Even unbelievers get foxhole religion! But only one man, or actually a boy, dared to *declare* God in the situation. The man *declaring* God changed the world of that moment.

God affirmed this teaching moment to David by serving up Goliath's head, and David never stopped declaring him. *David was so caught up in God that he actually saw himself as the personification of the will of God.* In other words, he recognized that he (like all of us) had a role to play and that the full faith and credit of the living God backed him up. Most notably, when David cries out to God regarding a "just cause," that just cause was *himself* (Ps. 17). That theme of considering himself a "just cause" in the eyes of God permeates the David's psalms. He knew who he was in God and he knew the regard God has for that.

> "Hear a just cause, O Lord, attend unto my cry."
>
> —Psalm 17:1

> "You have tested my heart . . . You have tried me and found nothing . . . Keep me as the apple of Your eye."
>
> —Psalm 17:3, 8

> "When I cry out to You, then my enemies will turn back; this I know because God is for me."
>
> —Psalm 56:9

> "He delivered me because He delighted in me . . . The Lord renewed me according to my righteousness; according to the cleanness of my hands He has recompensed me."
>
> —Psalm 18:19–20

It is hard to envision someone saying things like that today while keeping a straight face. *Yet we are sons and daughters of the Ruler of the Universe*, adopted into a *supernatural* family. David knew when he was being a righteous man in God's sight, just as today we are made righteous by our faith in the shed blood of our Lord and brother Jesus. We also know when we are walking holy before God with clean hands and a pure heart. David made declaration out of his awareness of who he was in God, and so should we.

If we made declarations like David's today, most Christians would probably expect a holy referee in a striped shirt to jump out, throw a flag and yell "foul!" Truth be told, we are often more into our unworthiness than into God's glory. Indeed, we were just poor sinners saved by grace, but saved we are, and Jesus believed us worthy enough to die a humiliating death on our behalf. We should not denigrate our Lord's death and love by believing he doesn't enjoy our boasting about him. We should declare him in the midst of every situation, particularly those situations where we know God's character well enough to know his views on a given subject. As I heard a pastor once say, "The gospel without power is *not* good news!" God is all about love and one expression of that is in divine power. "Now to Him who is able to do

A M A Z I N G L Y   G R A C E D

exceedingly abundantly above all that we ask or think, *according to the power that works in us, to Him be glory* in the church by Christ Jesus to all generations, forever and ever. Amen" (Eph. 3:20–21).

David's psalms are bursting with holy arrogance, the sort of declaration that would likely draw criticism today, and not just from an unbelieving public. It would draw criticism from our brethren as well. Yet God exalted a humble man who made arrogant boasts about him, declared him a man after his own heart, and *continues* to search out the Davids of today. God is glorified by our unfettered and unabashed declarations of him.

I make petition all the time to God, asking for help in all sorts of things. To be honest, sometimes I stick to petition-type prayers because I don't have the courage—not to mention the faith—to make declaration-type prayers. Sometimes this is just plain out of fear, fear that God won't show up or fear that someone will think me a nut. When I do that I know I am engaging in something more like *weenie* prayer rather than *warrior* prayer. But, bit by bit, I'm working on my self-esteem in God, and with increasing frequency, when I have a pretty good idea of what my heavenly Dad's position is on something, I'll step out and declare him. I want him to think I have a strong case of heavenly audacity. Nothing pops a father's buttons faster than when his kid is bragging about him. Especially when he knows his child is correct in the matter. *I would rather God believe I think too much of Him than too little.* I stand in increasing awe of the fact that the more I step out and declare him, the more God shows up and shows off.

David had a major handle on what makes God proud. It was on his heart and on his lips. We are what we speak. Life and death are still in the power of the tongue.[7]

The "Much More" of God

Here is another thought on the pursuit of heart—have you ever wondered what God has in mind for you in this pursuit?

It is a telling moment in the Bible when David is getting a holy chewing out by God over his having committed both adultery and murder. God sent His prophet Nathan to deliver the blistering message.

I anointed you king over Israel, and I delivered you from the hand of Saul. I gave you your master's house and your master's wives into your keeping and gave you the house of Israel and Judah. And if that had been too little, I also would have given you much more!

—2 Samuel 12:7–8

The message goes on outlining the very bad news for David and what was coming for his grand stupidity. But did you catch that one phrase: "And if that had been too little, I also would have given you much more!" In his hot anger, *God is spilling the beans of his heart*, doing his own little confession of what is the desire of *his* heart for those who dare to love him extravagantly. He is the God of "much more," not "less than." He wants us to experience the richness of his lovingkindness.[8] He wants you to be encouraged to step out into deeper places, places perhaps you have been hesitant to step. You are of great value to the Father. He actually considers *you* to be an incredible inheritance.[9]

He *wants* you to live in the place of his "much more." You should never, ever settle for less than what he wants to give you.

CHAPTER SIX

THAT'S *MISTER* HEAD
HONCHO TO YOU, PAL

*In the Kingdom, there are no great men of God, just humble men
whom God has chosen to use greatly.*
—Francis Frangipane

I first joined the Oklahoma County District Attorney's office as an
intern in law school. After graduation, I spent the next two years as
an assistant DA in that office. The good news was that I had a great
two years. After a short four months as a misdemeanor prosecutor,
I had tried four jury trials and only lost one. Then I tried nineteen
straight trials as a felony prosecutor—everything from shoplifting to
homicide—and never lost. Guilty, guilty, guilty was all I heard. Then
began the bad news. Somewhere along the line, I started thinking I was
the smartest guy in the world. I was king of the mountain and master
of my own destiny. When I left the office in the summer of 1983, my
fellow assistants even gave me a plaque declaring me "A True Winner."

God and I had a kind of strange relationship at the time. To me, God
was kind of like the goofy uncle that you want to keep away from your
friends but you can't completely kick him out of your life because he is
your mom's brother. I did my best to ignore the Divine Nudge. But for
some reason during law school, I found myself peeking at a Bible from
time to time. At least I remember having one in the trailer where I was

living. I really don't even remember why. I certainly hadn't darkened the door of a church for years. I think it was more superstition than anything else. Kind of like a talisman, keeping "The Book" close warded off evil spirits or something. Maybe I subconsciously thought its aura made me spiritual, operating like the "Force" in the mega-hit movie of that era, "Star Wars." I suspect a lot of people mistakenly liken God to the "Force," as though good and evil are on some sort of equal footing and we don't know who wins until the final episode. I just remember there being a total disconnect between God, the Bible, and my life. God was simply not personal to me. He was just this distant, negative, judgmental relative that you didn't really want to bring up in mixed company for fear you might not be accepted by your peers. In this odd period of God-dabbling, I would even hurl off a prayer before my jury trials. Why I'm not sure. Insurance maybe, just in case he was really real.

As I write this, I find myself drawn to a memory that somewhat exemplifies where I was spiritually and mentally during that period before God managed to get that moment of my time. Once again it involves my close friend, John Dwyer—but this was the John of an earlier era. Six foot five and larger than life, he was a college wild man and guided missile out for a good time. I recall sitting in the library of my mother's house (where I lived during my first tenure at the DA's office) talking on the phone with John and we were delving into the deeper things of life (which generally revolved around our egos and relationships with women). We were discussing what we wanted out of life. I'll never forget saying, "I want to be the head honcho of the biggest entity possible!" It really didn't matter what it was or whether I was qualified, of course, I just wanted to be The Man. It was all about me.

Pride—the Great God Repellant

> For thus says the High and Lofty One Who inhabits eternity, whose name is Holy: "I dwell in the high and holy place, with him who has a contrite and humble spirit, to revive the spirit of the humble, and to revive the heart of the contrite ones."
> —Isaiah 57:15

And I will be even more undignified than this and will be
humble in my own sight.

—David in 2 Samuel 6:22

As I quoted in the opening principle associated with this chapter,
Francis Frangipane once said, "In the Kingdom, there are no great men
of God, just humble men whom God has chosen to use greatly."[1] I wish
I had coined that phrase. It is incredibly correct. There is nothing that
acts like God-repellant better than a good case of pride. The Bible is
replete with examples. A prideful person sees little or no need in God
because they are largely self-absorbed and unteachable. This obviously
comes in varying degrees, because many of us as Christians have blind
spots where pride reigns.

Pride has always been my arch-nemesis. Me and about a billion other
men, so at least I'm not alone. It pops up in the most interesting places,
places I would not have necessarily considered a matter of so-called
"pride." I always used to think of pride as being a haughty, obvious sort
of activity, like bragging, mirror watching, refusals to apologize, being
stuck up—that sort of thing. Certainly it can be that but it is much
more. Where it is insidious and especially dangerous is when it comes
masked as *embarrassment*. I am convinced this strain of pride is a major
cancer in the body of Christ today.

In April of 2003, Lori and I were vacationing in Aruba. Before we
were married, Lori had been an avid windsurfer, but after we married
she pretty much quit for years. We chose Aruba because Lori wanted
to resume the sport again and the island's constant wind and relatively
shallow bay made it a great place to do so. The shallow aspect was
important, as Lori tended to be distracted at the thought of deeper
water creatures viewing her as dinner.

While there, I decided I would give windsurfing a whirl. I am not
a very good swimmer, and like all beginning windsurfers I managed
to fall off the board with some frequency while learning balance and
control of the sail board. Life vests were available. However, I looked
out on the water and saw virtually nobody wearing a life vest. So, I was
embarrassed at the thought of being a forty-eight year old manly-man
wearing a girly-man life vest. I took the lessons and finally started to
get in the groove, leaning back in the harness and letting the wind

fill the sail, propelling me swiftly across the saltwater in a delicious intersection of sea, sun and speed. It was exhilarating.

I let the wind hurl me along in something like hundred yard sailing sprints, which is about all the distance I could go before my inexperience would drive me off the board and into the water. It was especially comforting to fall off and be only three or four feet above a sandy bottom. Again and again I would get back on the board, both of my hands tightly clenching the sail's boom, leaning well back away from the sail with only the harness and my white knuckled hands keeping me from falling back into the water. Every time the wind would gust, the sail would fight to wrench itself out of my grasp. The wind was fuel powering my sail. I began to experiment, allowing my right hand to release pressure on the sail ever so slightly, allowing the sail to pull away a few degrees and then pull it back, release and pull, release and pull. Every pull on the sail toward me was like revving the engine of the board and it would scream forward just a little bit faster.

This whole mechanism of windsurfing was nowhere approaching second nature, and I concentrated hard to bring all the puzzle pieces of speed and balance together. My concentration on the mechanics meant I was not paying attention to how far away from the shallow bay I was getting. Suddenly, finally, a brief, violent gust of wind jerked the sail out of my hands and my extreme backward lean jettisoned me off the back of the board. The water's impact at first felt cool and refreshing as I plunged beneath the surface and quickly rose back up for air. This time my feet had not touched sand. They hadn't touched anything solid at all. I opened my eyes just in time to see that the sail had lodged on the board in such a way that it did not fall into the water but remained up and able to catch wind. Helplessly, I watched my board sail away from me out to sea. It was the beginning of a bad dream. As I clumsily dogpaddled, I could feel the nothingness of the water beneath my feet. There was no comforting sandy bottom of the shallow bay, and no simply *standing up* to save myself from drowning. My heart rate lurched upward as I looked to see that I was probably a couple of hundred yards from shore. I had never swum that far in my life.

Other windsurfers barreled along back and forth all around me and I could feel myself getting winded as I swam against the wind toward the shore. Every now and again I would stop and poke my foot downward to see if I had gone far enough for my feet to touch the bottom. But there was no such luck, even though I could easily see the bottom through the clear water. It might as well have been a hundred feet deep. As I grew more tired, I started trying to get the attention of passing windsurfers but they were too far into the moment of wind and sail to notice my flailing arms. It was so unreal—they were having a magnificent time as I was getting ready to drown in their exuberant wake. I was now quickly running out of energy and feeling the edge of panic. Literally on the verge of exhaustion, I spotted a fellow beginner about fifty yards away. He had seen my circumstance and was so-very-slowly making his way over to me. He was one of those very cautious beginners who made a point of moving along the surface of the water at what seemed barely a creep. As I struggled to keep afloat (I wasn't even a decent dogpaddler), my own panic became coupled to the growing fear that he would suddenly slip and fall off the board and thus affirm my doom. Couldn't he move faster than an inch an hour? Still he puttered my way, bit by bit, gut wrenching inch by inch. I was very nearly in a state of collapse when he got close enough for me to grasp the edge of his board. He saved my life.

I feel inadequate right now expressing the depth of emotion with which I was smitten as I walked up the beach toward the hotel. It had been my first and only brush with death. I have this vivid memory of eating dinner at a restaurant that night, sitting, staring down at my plate full of food, my eyes moist from the terrifying memory of the day. I just kept thinking, *I really, truly nearly died today.* That afternoon God gave me a very clear message about my pride. I don't recall at what exact point he spoke to my heart—on the beach, in the hotel room, wherever—but it was crystal clear and that still small voice struck like a hammer. It was but a simple phrase I heard as clearly as the waiter asking my order at dinner, *Wes, if you are so arrogant that you will not wear a life vest, I will let you die.*

I am not sure I had ever equated arrogance with embarrassment until God pointed it out to me that day. As I've said before, one way you get a clue that you are truly hearing God speak is that what he says is way too smart to have come from your own head. Plus, if it also points you toward repentance then it is a virtual guarantee whose voice it was you just heard.

Just Call Me "PC"

The pride I displayed in Aruba is the same pride that has plagued me throughout my walk of faith. It is a form of pride that is both external and internal. In other words, it is the embarrassment I have displayed externally in secular public, and the embarrassment I have displayed internally in the company of fellow believers. From an external perspective, my pride challenge has been displayed when I am acting pretty much like a "secret agent" for God. At times I am so embarrassed about being a Christian that I treat God like that goofy uncle I referred to earlier, rather than someone with whom I am privileged to associate. This form of pride treats God as someone to be kept in the closet and spoken of in only hushed tones.

For a long time I was a very effective secret agent for God. Nobody at work had a clue I was a Christian. In fact, I was probably so good at this secret agent shtick that not even God knew I was working for him. Now *that's* good! Let's face it; I had bought into all the political correctness garbage. It was simply not "PC" to be an overt Christian. I suspect Jesus was not overly pleased with my conduct, what with having died for me and all. I would pretend I was just trying to be sensitive to the feelings of others, but truth be known, I was embarrassed to be identified with Jesus in public. It just was not cool. It was PC to be a nut about football or fishing, but not about God.

Fortunately, I had men in my life who were opposing forces to my pride, men who held me accountable on my shortcomings and demanded I "man up" about what I believed. Men like Bob Potter, who used to drive me absolutely crazy. He would call me every few weeks and want to go to lunch. I used to dread getting his phone messages because I knew he would be asking me if I had shared my faith with anyone lately. Not necessarily share like "Do you know Jesus?" but just by showing people you care about them and, if the opportunity arose, to be willing to share my faith in Christ. It was not a hunt for spiritual scalps but more of lifestyle evangelism. It was not like the time in college when a red headed wild man spun around and confronted me while we were alone in an elevator with a loud "are you saved?" It was more just being as willing to casually talk about Jesus as I was about my favorite actor. I had always dreaded that thought like the plague. Bob was relentless but kind, and deep down I knew he was right. He and others gently prodded me along, bit by bit, as I slowly overcame being what Hugh Hewitt once referred to as "The Embarrassed Believer"—in other words, an American Christian.[2] I will always be grateful to Bob for his prickly persistence. It changed my life.

My friend, John Dwyer, used to embarrass me greatly when we would go out to eat at a restaurant. This, of course, was in his "post-pagan" era. He would always insist on praying over the meal. I would die a thousand deaths as he would pray. It seemed like the prayers lasted forever. I could feel scores of eyes boring in on us as he seemed to pray for everything under the sun. Couldn't he just stick to thanking God for the meal and be done with it? I would sort of tease him by saying, "Okay, John, let's keep it under twenty minutes." In reality, his prayers probably lasted less than a minute, but they felt like an eternity. What radically changed my point of view on the subject was when my sister had lunch with John one day and came back to report that an amazing thing had taken place during the lunch. John also drove her nuts with his insisting on praying, but this time, about midway through the lunch, an elderly man came up to the table. It seems that he had observed John praying with Dianne. The man was taking a break while his wife was in a nearby hospital. She was not doing well and he was very discouraged. He commented that he was so deeply moved by watching them pray that it had given him the strength to go back to the hospital and face their situation! I was blown away. I had been so caught up in *me* and *my* embarrassment that it never dawned on me that someone might actually be blessed by my willingness to not be embarrassed about having a relationship with God.

Just Wear the Vest

To my knowledge, David never had a problem with this sort of "external" embarrassment. "I will declare Your name to my brethren, in the midst of the assembly I will praise You" (Ps. 22:22). And Jesus had a pretty strong comment on the subject: "But whoever denies Me before men, him I will also deny before My Father who is in heaven" (Matt. 11:33).

As I have pondered it, I think God's comment to me in Aruba was about a lot more than wearing a life vest. He was letting me know there was a principle associated with my embarrassment, and that principle was my lack of humility. God loves me a lot, but if I valued my pride more than my life by not wearing a life vest when I knew I needed one, he would not stand in the way of my self-destruction. So goes it with the pride surrounding being embarrassed about my relationship with him. Although God has a meaningful and significant destiny for our lives, and we may deeply desire that and even pray for it, he will not let us grow any further into that destiny than our pride will allow. If our pride is an impediment to what God wants to do with us, and if we are unwilling to deal with that, he is perfectly willing to allow us to miss out on his best for our lives. *He will not overrule our free will.* Our lack of humility—pride—has the ability to both kill us physically and kill God's best for our lives. It is all our choice. "God resists the proud, but gives grace to the humble" (James 4:6).

People Pleasing Never Does

Before I move on to a different realm of embarrassment and pride, Lori felt strongly I need to mention another externalized brand of pride that is insidious, deadly, and commonly mistaken for anything *but* pride. In fact, as Lori puts it, this subtle form of pride masquerades as "being a nice person." She says, "When you think you can please people or make them happy, you are suffering from a most damaging form of pride. To think you are powerful enough to bring joy and happiness into their lives says you are more powerful than a normal person, or more powerful than the person you are trying to please. In reality, you are not in control of what anybody thinks or feels. You can only control yourself."

Lori knows what she's talking about. This form of pride nearly killed her as she found herself caught up in a facial plastic surgery practice where her entire self worth was wrapped up in the ability to please other people and make them happy. She wanted to be perfect for everybody, and that perfection depended upon everyone else's state of happiness. The more she ran into unhappy people who were driven by their own self esteem issues to seek surgery (not everyone was like this of course), the more her own self esteem took a brutal beating. She found herself able only to change their outward appearance, but not their heart. It was a vicious, impossible, and deadly cycle that contributed to her turning to self medication with drugs and later alcohol.

It is one thing to want to serve people and another to think you can control their feelings. One is a gifting from God, the other a lie from hell. If we find our effort to serve others has a spirit of control or manipulation intermingled with it, we need to repent because that "servant's heart" is a thing of pride and will kill you off just as surely as refusing to wear a life vest on the high seas. We have plenty enough to do dealing with our own hearts, much less changing everyone else's. Leave that to God.

Will the Real Pharisee Please Stand Up?

Finally, as I said, there was another form of embarrassment. This is the internal absence of humility I occasionally display amongst my fellow believers, an example of which manifested in my worship. God has been dealing with me for years on this. I am very much improved on the subject, especially after God's little comment in Aruba.

When I first attended a church at which people raised their hands in worship back in the early 1990s, I was offended and appalled. I guess I had missed somewhere that his people in the Bible did that routinely. It was just so dramatic, so *loose*. But as I examined my heart on the matter I began to see that the reason I was offended was because I was actually embarrassed at the thought of being seen doing that myself. It had nothing to do with my being offended *for* God. It was all about *me*. Engaging in that sort of behavior would have been demeaning to *me*. It was beneath *me*. It looked goofy and immature to *me*. I suspect that I am not the only one who has suffered from this delusion. A lot of people get jammed up over the way their brothers and sisters worship. Their response is to criticize, just as I did. Sure, there are some folks that go over the edge and are really seeking a bit of attention, but I figure that God can sort that out and doesn't need me to be the Worship Police for him. I suspect he has a bigger problem with me being offended out of my pharisaical pride than with someone dancing before his throne for the wrong motive.

In the interest of full disclosure, I also know that part of the revulsion I had for another believer's form of worship was rooted not in embarrassment but in a more traditional, pharisaical pride. That critical, prideful spirit that grips us whenever we are confronted by our "less spiritual" neighbors, those Christians who we know God loves but surely frowns upon (since we have the right doctrine and they obviously do not). I looked down my nose at these people worshiping not only because I was embarrassed but because I smugly knew that I was more enlightened spiritually than were they. Boy, I bet that made my heavenly Father proud.

David had a pretty good handle on this subject and he has been my twelve-step program for dealing with pride in many arenas. David's rebuttal to his wife Michal's criticism was "and I will be even more undignified than this and will be humble in my own sight" (2 Sam. 6:22).[3] He was very ready to be "undignified" in his worship. Here he was—the king of Israel—and he was more than willing to appear the fool for God. His Pharisee-like wife got all puffed up over how he made quite the scene ditching his kingly robes and dancing feverishly in a simple ephod (a shortened priestly garment) while leading a procession bearing the Ark of the Covenant. To the furious Michal it was all about her and what people would think. From her point of view he might as well have been leading a drunken Mardi Gras parade while break dancing in his underwear. Michal missed the whole point. She was all caught up in her pride and personal dignity while David was all caught up in God.

God's great desire to see to our success comes at the expense of our pride. One cannot help but wonder how many countless Christians over the centuries have come up short in reaping the benefit of God's great pleasure because they just could never get past their pride. In contrast, I suspect that if God had given David the command to dance in his underwear in the middle of a Jerusalem marketplace at high noon (and God throughout the Bible has ordered some pretty wild things of his children—see for example Isaiah 20), David, out of his profound understanding that God always has loving purpose behind even the oddest directives, would have been more than pleased to abandon every last shred of public dignity.

For me, it is a long trip from wanting to be the head honcho of the biggest entity possible to being willing to do the embarrassing before God. Or at least it continues to be since it's a trip I've not yet completed. The trip from pride is not easy and may even be a life-long journey, since I—we—insist on returning so often. But the escape vehicle is the *willingness to be willing*. Being willing to be willing means our reluctant but volitional compliance with God's processes. "I'm scared to death, Lord, about what is on the road ahead. I am reluctant to walk this path because of my fear. But if you can do a work in me, I am willing to be willing." We are not all zealous warriors, frothing at the mouth to do God's bidding. Some of us know we would like to be more dedicated in our pursuit of God, but whatever our impediment, we cannot make that transition on our own. God understands that and it is enough for us to tell him we are willing to be willing. He knows how to respond to sincerity.

Most of us desire a deeper, more vibrant relationship with God. Figuratively speaking, what stands in the way of that is our unwillingness to break dance in our underwear before the Lord of Hosts. In other words, the willingness to be shed, bit by bit, of the things that are obstacles to that depth of relationship for which we long. For me, and for many of us, that obstacle is pride. I hold onto my pride dearly, and it is difficult to fully and permanently step away from it. For others, it might be something else to which you cling. Ultimately, it is only in our love for God and our longing to deepen our love relationship with a supernatural God that we release our grip on that which holds us back. Experiencing the depths of relationship with God is all about learning how to let go and dance before the Ark of the Lord, because nothing else really matters anymore than that.

God help me that someday I would love the Lord so much that I, like David, would not be too proud to break dance in my underwear for him.

PART III
THE ATMOSPHERE OF FAITH

God shows up in many ways. Sometimes he does so in the spectacular, and sometimes he just does. He is so very patient and understanding. He is the looming, loving parent beneath whose shadow we sometimes walk at times unaware. He meets us at the point where our faith dwells—however meager the housing—always prepared to lead us into better accommodations when we are ready for the move.

CHAPTER SEVEN

HEALED

God has long dealt with doubters and, fortunately, he is imminently patient with us. He so wants to help us work our way through our unbelief. Working through it also determines the extent to which we will realize the amazing destiny he has for each of us. He meets us where we are and will encourage us on this path, so long as we keep seeking him.

It was October of 2001. I had only been District Attorney for three months when I got word that the Oklahoma Bureau of Narcotics had launched an investigation of my wife, Lori. Not long afterwards, the Attorney General's office filed charges against her.

By the mid 1990s, Lori had become a very successful facial plastic surgeon. This former Miss Oklahoma would appear routinely in the media. Not just on local television, she was consistently featured in national magazines and even national television. She appeared on everything from the Today Show to segments of 20/20®, Geraldo, Sally Jesse, and other national programs of the time. She was a national spokesperson for Collagen, and she was being groomed to be one for Botox as well, having even been sent to New York for media training. She graced the magazine covers of "Today's Christian Woman" and Guidepost's "Clarity." "Vanity Fair®" magazine named her one of the

"200 most influential women in America." What started as her personal ministry of providing free cosmetic surgery to battered and disfigured victims of domestic violence had mushroomed into the national "Face to Face" program with the American Academy of Facial Plastic and Reconstructive Surgeons. Hundreds of surgeons participated all across North America.

As Lori puts it, "I had a successful practice and marriage, was slim and had all the cute clothes, but I still wasn't happy at my core. I was extremely thankful to the Lord but all this was not translating into joy—something I was seeing in other Christians. I was trying to make everything okay, even if it wasn't. I would go to great lengths to explain it all away to myself. I so wanted everything to be just right. But where was the joy?"

The Bible speaks clearly about joy being a by-product of an obedient walk with God.[1] As Lori's inexplicable unhappiness became clearer, we went before the Lord one night in our living room and began petitioning him that Lori would experience that which had been promised but was missing.

We cannot recall exactly when it was that Lori started experiencing back pain, but she started seeking medical treatment in 1997. Upon getting a CT scan, she learned she had compressed vertebrae in what is referred to as the C3 to C6 region of her spine (upper back). These compressed vertebrae were pinching on the nerves radiating out from her spine, resulting in ever escalating degrees of pain. She also began to lose strength and sensation in her right hand (the hand with which she used to operate as a surgeon). The really bad news was that her doctor did not believe that back surgery would be particularly effective, and, sounding the death knell of a successful medical practice, made the comment, "I hope you have disability insurance."

Lori started receiving treatment by way of steroids, physical therapy, and a prescription for hydrocodone to help endure the increasing pain. The two steroid treatments and physical therapy did nothing to ultimately solve the problem, and so she started taking more and more of the pills to cope with the pain and ultimately to keep up with all the demands. In her own words,

I began experiencing night sweats and fatigue, as well as other symptoms. I thought it might be either menopause or even chronic fatigue syndrome. But I was not sleeping and would go to work many days with only a couple of hours of sleep. I was finding I could not finish the day at the same pace I needed to in order to keep up with all the demands. I was booked six months to a year ahead for consultations and surgery. I discovered that a side effect of the hydrocodone was a sense of renewed energy. I began to take the drug to keep pace with the demands. I didn't even feel guilty about it because at that time of my life I had convinced myself that the way I pleased God was by getting all my work done and pleasing my patients, even if it killed me.

In the meantime, I was trying to figure out what was wrong with me and why was I so horribly fatigued. I was going to several doctors and even traveling to Palm Desert, California, to a rejuvenation clinic. I also went down to Sulphur, Oklahoma, to a health and wellness center. The only thing keeping me going was the hydrocodone. I could take one of those pills and finish my day, all the while believing God must be very pleased.

But even with the drugs, the pain in Lori's back kept escalating, and by the spring of 1999, the drugs were ultimately ineffective in turning off the pain.

Journal: Sunday, April 11, 1999

Last week was pretty, no quite, profound. It began last Sunday when Lori, Derrick, Mom, and I wound up having lunch with the Everett Cox's and the Frank Porter's. I saw Frank around at church and I suppose I sensed something about him. It became clear during lunch that he, like Pat Ward, has a deep and abiding relationship with the Lord. Now a few years back I would have had a real hard time accepting what I heard. Perhaps not so much at this point. There has been too much water under the bridge as they say. Frank works with Everett in deliverance ministry. For some months now I have been asking the Lord to "max me out" in my relationship with him. I want to fully experience him and to access everything he has for one of the Kingdom kids. George Müller, Bill Gothard, and many others have had a profound impact from God's direct working in their lives—and I have wanted more of that for mine.

Frank invited Lori and me to his class the next night. He was winding up classes on teaching ministry teams in deliverance and would be recapping a few things. It turned out we were able to be there and Frank felt led of God to pray for us as a couple. He called for folks to lay hands on Lori's back (I don't think he knew of her problem). Then he pulled me aside [afterward] and told me the Lord directed him to tell me that I had "doubts." I wish I could recall exactly what he said, but it was essentially that the Lord knew I had doubts beneath the surface that needed to be addressed.

Now this baffled me. Here I was, Mr. Bold and Courageous, going around teaching people [at Christian men's group meetings and the like] to remember that God has not changed and that he would take care of everything. Me, have doubts? Ridiculous! In my puffed up pride I told Frank that that totally baffled me.

On the way home (we had taken separate cars), I can only say that I was reflecting with the Lord my confusion on that matter when it was as if something lifted the lid on a garbage can making me realize that Frank was right. In fact I was awash in doubt about certain things of God. Not that God existed, or about Jesus or anything like that, but I guess doubts about God's willingness to carry out everything he says he will. Maybe especially about his willingness to take me where I am hoping to go spiritually, and maybe about his willingness to really heal Lori. I was smitten by guilt at this realization. God had exposed my iniquity. I couldn't even really point out some of my doubts too specifically, just that they were abounding in such a way as to make me feel something of a faker. It's kind of hard to explain really, because I feel so strongly about Müller and Gothard. Yet, as I sit here, I think it might be doubt that God will do those same things for me. I am reminded of the time Jesus asked a man if he believed. The man said "Yes, Lord, I believe, help me in my unbelief."

I felt let down with myself. I didn't know how on earth I was going to resolve this doubt. Very frustrated and sad.

I vividly remember sitting there that April evening while being prayed for by Pastor Frank and the others. I recall looking over at Lori sitting next to me. She had her eyes tightly shut and kept saying, "I'm standing on my being healed." She was choosing to believe that she was being healed. I was just trying to keep my jaw up and off the floor what with the boisterous prayer going on around us. At one point those praying started a sort of whooping and hollering, one person calling out, "Boy, did you feel that?" as if they sensed something had taken place in the spiritual atmosphere. All I knew at the time was that I wasn't feeling squat. But Lori was standing firm on something upon which I could only gawk.

I was so offended when Pastor Frank let me know my private thoughts were not my own in the realm of the Holy Spirit. "The Lord tells me you have doubt," he said, towering over me. I felt my religious pride kick in, mentally embracing my Christian speaking schedule and how I was such a great encourager to the Christian troops—as if I had no room for improvement myself. I was feeling rather confident about my walk with God, wanting more to be sure, but all the same a wee bit smug at what a great Christian I thought I was. The very fact that I was immediately offended by the truth exposed how utterly minor league my faith actually was.

I was despondent realizing the depth of my doubt; how empty the reservoir of my faith. I had sincerely prayed God would "max me out" on my faith, only to learn that he had actually taken my request seriously.

Wrestling Doubt

Journal: Sunday, April 18, 1999

I never got to finish my notes last week. It was quite intense as I thought I was going to be in trial, and that can be an incredible distraction. To continue, as it happened (through the Lord's provision), the group from Hope's Harbor

Church was taking me to lunch the Thursday after the Monday night revealing to me of all my doubts. This group has been so kind to me. They bring cookies to my staff [in the Juvenile Division] over Christmas and pray regularly for Lori and me. I met them for lunch and in attendance were Pastor Kerry Freeman, Nita Patton, Kay Wheeler, and Joe Mowdy. Interestingly enough, I was supposed to have had lunch with them a week earlier but there was a scheduling foul-up and couldn't. Praise God this was delayed, because a week ago I didn't have any issues. The Lord is very generous in his provision. Kay and Joe were quite profound in their ministry to me. They made it clear that this doubt issue was a matter for the Lord's power to resolve and for me to release the guilt over it. They encouraged me to put on the armor of God. Essentially, they let me know that this battle was not mine, and that gave me a great sense of comfort and release. The truly profound thing was they made it clear this was actually God answering my prayer! For some time I had been praying that the Lord would draw me closer to him and, as Kay put it, in order to do this God had to increase the intensity of the "light" on me to expose issues that needed resolution. Wow! I had not even considered this. He was lifting the lid on my garbage can in answer to my own prayer in order that issues might be addressed so that our relationship might be all the closer. The very revelation brought tears to my eyes and great relief. God in his provision had arranged this lunch period in advance so I might be ministered to on this issue. I pray, O God, that you will wash away these doubts in my life in order that I might be closer to you and fully receive all that you have for me and that I might glorify you all the greater.

It was over the next few weeks that Lori's pain started easing up and she began regaining strength. Then, as if nothing had ever been a problem, the pain stopped, the numbness ended, full strength returned. Her back was completely and totally healed! At some point upon reporting Lori's complete recovery to the pastors, we were warned that things were not necessarily over and that we needed to be aware that at times Satan, who authors attacks on our health, may well come back and attempt to "rob Lori of her healing." This was a new one on me and just another thought I was struggling to completely get my skeptical head around. But, on the other hand, how could I get around the fact that we had already witnessed a medical miracle? It would be several months before we came face to face with a bizarre and once unbelievable event that would serve to both highlight and underscore the existence of an unseen realm within which prowls our deadly Enemy and his minions.

Another Dead Doubt

Late in the night, two days before Christmas of 1999, Lori was awakened from her sleep in severe back and neck pain. She lay in bed for at least a couple of hours praying and hoping it would go away. When she got out of bed, she found that once again her right hand felt severely weakened and she was unable to even turn the sink faucet handle with that hand. It was all coming back, all the pain and physical infirmity from which she had suffered but which had been missing for months. She finally awakened me.

I was a bit further down the spiritual trail than I had been the preceding spring when God initially healed Lori's back and exposed my nagging doubts. The Crider case had stretched my faith. I had seen supernatural responses from a supernatural God. My skepticism had been severely damaged from that event. As I came out of my grogginess, I snapped to the fact that this may be what we were warned about concerning Satan's crowd coming back to reclaim lost territory. I couldn't be sure, but exactly what were our choices? Go back to the doctor to once again be told the matter was pretty much hopeless? There was only one option.

As Lori sat in great pain on the side of the bed, I decided on a course of action that once upon a time I would have thought completely nuts. I began to speak out, commanding the Devil or demons to depart! I kept repeating this over and over, binding them in the name of Jesus, rebuking their presence, pleading the blood of Jesus at the cross and commanding them to leave. In short, I took authority over the situation.[2] Then the real weirdness began. We knew I was hitting proverbial pay dirt and that I was actually addressing a *being* when the pain began to *severely increase as I commanded it to go*! It was as though something was twisting a knife in a desperate bid to maintain its claim. Then suddenly, the pain disappeared. It did not dissipate or slowly subside. It departed *instantaneously*. One second there was intense, wracking pain, and the next second it was like nothing had happened at all. The pain was completely gone and like a shot, it was over. As we sat there in the wee hours of the morning we could only marvel in stunned amazement at what had taken place. It was one of those "I-would-not-have-believed-it-but-for-the-fact-I-was-there-and-saw-it" moments. But the battle was not over.

Late the very next night, Christmas Eve, it started all over again. This time as Lori lay in *intense* pain she actually debated *not* waking me up because on the previous night, the pain had become virtually unbearable as I began addressing it. Finally, her restlessness sitting on the edge of the bed awakened me and I immediately became aware of what was afoot. This time there was no hesitation concerning what step to take and I once again began to bind the attacker in the name of Jesus, commanding it to depart. Again and again I spoke that, and again and again the knife of pain ratcheted up unmercifully on Lori. Then, finally, SNAP! It departed. The pain was *instantly and totally* gone. It was all like something out of a B movie, except that we had both seen and experienced this. It was for real.

Since the Crider case, we had been reading up on the subject of spiritual warfare.[3] After this second attack, we decided to pull another tool from our bag of spiritual weaponry and asked the Lord to establish a "hedge of protection" around our bedroom. The pain never returned and to this day, Lori's back has never troubled her again.

Round 2

Interestingly enough, the same omnipotent God that so graciously healed Lori's back in 1999, chose *not* to immediately remove the drug addiction that had ensnared her as she sought relief from the pain. We were still dealing with that Christmas bedroom enemy, yet God had a plan to deal with him and had not forgotten the prayer we still had on the table concerning Lori's missing joy.

A few months later, during the summer of 2000, I was sitting on our back porch when Lori stepped outside to join me. Something was clearly wrong. Her mascara was running down her cheeks. This itself was a rare event as I had only seen Lori cry a very few times. She told me that she had just been confronted by her medical staff. They had been noticing some aberrant behavior ultimately concluding, correctly, that she had been abusing narcotics. She admitted she had become addicted to the prescription given her for the back pain, and despite being physically healed she had remained hooked on the drug. She was despondent.

I was stunned. Usually when one thinks of drug or alcohol abusers one thinks of wild behavior such as crazy mood swings, weaving cars, slurred speech, and stumbling walk. Lori exhibited none of that. She was acting like a couple of lawyers I knew at the courthouse who were reputed to be "functioning alcoholics," people who for a time appear to be just fine but abusing all the same. I actually had a relative like that. He seemed perfectly normal. He would farm his land, work his other business and fly his plane. He seemed to have a can of beer in his hand a lot, but I didn't think much of it. A lot of people drank beer. Someone said he had a drinking problem but to me and others, he always seemed to be perfectly normal, so in control. After he flew his plane into the ground and killed himself, it was a little late for anyone to help him with the then apparent addiction. Lloyd had been an alcoholic. But on the surface he seemed to do everything so well.

But Lori wasn't drinking like that. She might have an occasional glass of wine, but at the time that was as far as she would go where alcohol was concerned. She certainly wasn't sharing the fact that she was raiding pills from the office narcotics cabinet to help her cope with her growing fatigue. Nonetheless, her crying presence on the back porch betrayed another harsh reality: I was completely out of touch with what was going on in my wife's life. We had become two career ships passing one another in the night. I had not been paying attention to the little things that might have been clues to what was going on. I was so focused on me that I was dropping the ball on my role as her husband.

After the staff intervention, she immediately got treatment with an Oklahoma City hospital's out-patient program. Some months later, when the medical licensure board required a routine annual form to be filled out, she honestly admitted to having gotten treatment. She had dropped the drugs cold turkey and we thought it was over. But God had a different plan. She was still in the midst of a demanding, people-pleasing practice that was poison to her emotionally and physically. There was still no joy. The Lord would have to strip that all away before there could be lasting healing.

When I first got word that the Bureau of Narcotics investigation had been launched on Lori, I was deeply in the throws of my new and tumultuous role as district attorney. The previous month of September, I had finally made my nationally televised announcement that I would be continuing the prosecution of Terry Nichols. It had been a wrenching summer of meeting with victims and family members of deceased victims of the Murrah Building bombing, as well as the new experience for me of dealing with the press and a very vocal public. Then there was the not-so-minor matter of just trying to get a grip on an office that filed thousands upon thousands of criminal cases every year, with a staff of one hundred and fifty legal professionals, all undergoing the first change of leadership in over twenty years. I also made the personally surprising discovery that change produces fear. Even though I had been an assistant in the office for some sixteen years, even though I got along famously with everyone and thought all would be just wonderful, there was more than a little drama taking place on the inside of the district attorney's office.

I got my first clue of the future loneliness of leadership when a longtime co-worker of whom I thought highly came to me and with obvious trepidation asked, "What shall we call you?" At first the question did not register. And then it became clear that she wanted to know if the staff should now call me "Mr. Lane." It was beginning to dawn on me that my relationships within the office would for the most part be forever changed. I was now the boss, with all its attendant power over the lives of my former fellow worker bees. I looked at my friend and simply smiled and responded cheerfully, "How about what I've always been called—Wes?"

The speed at which the collective experience was coming at me was much like the old saying of taking information through a fire hose. It was exciting but stressful just the same. But no drama was as great as the one coming down the pike at my quiet and kind wife.

There is nothing quite like learning a loved one is being investigated, especially when one is the so-called "minister of justice" (as the United States Supreme Court referred once to the role of district attorney) for one's community. There is the great stress of the waiting helplessly, knowing you cannot lift a finger or say a thing lest it be interpreted by some as official interference. It defies all that otherwise would work within a husband who wants to be protective of his wife. Yet that was all that I could do during the waiting period.

But even then, God performed a kindness.

I don't recall the date I received a phone call that the Attorney General would be filing charges against Lori. I just remember the numbness and the intensity of the stress that was roiling within me. At some point before this day, a group from the national Christian organization, Promise Keepers, had called and made an appointment to see me. I do not recall the reason they wanted to see me. I just remember that I was deeply frustrated that within an hour of having received the call concerning the charges, these folks were going to be in my office and I was going to have to smile and pretend that all was right with the world by saying, "How can I help you?" Had one of them not been from out of state, I would have cancelled the appointment. Yet, there they were in my office, happily sharing with me what they were up to and inside I was dying. For a while I kept up the pretense, nodding assurance and feigned interest. All smiles. But there was something very kind, good, and reassuring about them that kept exuding into the atmosphere within the room. Their love for God, their desire to help men accomplish a deeper walk with God—it overwhelmed me and finally I found myself desperately wanting to share with them what I was going through at that very moment. I couldn't take it any longer. I interrupted the conversation, told them about the phone call I had just received, and then I broke down and wept.

It is a remarkable thing when God orchestrates a meeting. I have now seen him do it many times by putting people and circumstances together at just the right and profound moment. In their kind, loving manner, this combination of men I barely knew ministered to me in a crucial moment of my grief for my wife. When I say *minister* I mean that they lovingly let me pour out my pain without judgment, kindly reminded me of God's love and sovereignty, and prayed for me and my family. It was a balm expertly applied, and one I had not even requested. God knew what I needed at that moment, long before the meeting. When they left, I was stronger for them having come. And I needed to be.

The Bureau of Narcotics and Attorney General's office were just doing their job. Still, the story that was a media dream became our nightmare. Typically, when a doctor deals with an addiction, the public never knows about it. But the wife of the district attorney was another issue. News of the charges even made *U.S.A. Today* and the *Los Angeles Times*. Like those in law enforcement, most of the media were just doing their job as well. Over the next several months, however, we would learn the difference between reporters simply doing their job and the ones that went above and beyond what was professional and ethical. One reporter I had naively believed to be so "nice" worked to have several of Lori's patients sue her, acquired an attorney for them, and then obtained supposed "exclusive" interviews with the "victims" (pretending to be reporting the news instead of *making* the news as this reporter was actually doing). All of which then ran during what is known as "sweeps week"[4] on the reporter's news station. It was our season from hell. But it was absolutely nothing for me compared to the pain it caused Lori. Lori, the one who always felt a deep need to both perform and please everyone so perfectly to feel accepted, was completely exposed as imperfect for the entire world to see. And, in a divine plan far beyond our comprehension, it was apparently exactly what needed to happen. We would certainly discover what Joseph of the Bible discovered when betrayed into slavery by his brothers, but later, in the experience's aftermath, could lovingly say to them in Genesis 50:20, "But as for you, you meant evil against me; but God meant it for good . . . ."

Journal: Saturday, November 17, 2001

I'm sitting in the easy chair this Saturday morning with Moose [another Italian Greyhound] licking the computer keyboard amidst a dog pretzel pile of Moose, Gnocchi and Ralph; all crammed in this chair with me as I try catching up with what has taken place over the last couple of weeks. It has been tumultuous to say the least.

When it became obvious that all of this about Lori was going to come out in public through the OBN [Oklahoma Bureau of Narcotics] and the Medical Board, we decided the only thing to do was to get out in front of it. After all, the reason the board and OBN knew about it in the first instance was because Lori had been honest in filling out their form.[5] To allow the press to set the agenda was to surrender to the sharks. We knew there would be a feeding frenzy because it was too juicy considering she is married to the DA. On Monday night, November 5th, we went public, traveling to the Daily Oklahoman and then making the rounds to the TV stations. Lori and I went on the air together and Lori told all about how the Lord healed her back in April of 1999, but not before she had become drug dependent. Well, to say the least, the frenzy ensued. Some stations were very kind. The rest, however, were another story and have had difficulty in telling the story accurately. Doing the stories themselves has not been the problem. We are fair game. I am a public figure. But at least a couple of times they put fallacious stuff on the air *knowing* the information was inaccurate.

Even in the midst of all this mess, I have enjoyed an over-riding sense of peace. My poor and precious Lori has understandably not been doing so well. The humiliation and shame she has been feeling is immense. She has had TV trucks parked outside her office and has been the subject of a number of trash stories. She hardly wants to show her face at the grocery store. Yet, I have never loved her more than over the last couple of weeks. She is a woman of such profound character. The Lord has so richly blessed me with her. There is a history now to the Lord's dealing with us. How many Christians have been privileged to see so much of the supernatural workings of the living God? I sit here and shake my head in wonderment over everything. Wow. I have prayed *knowing* that the Lord did not raise us up to have us appear as public fools and thus discredit himself. Our prayers for some time have been that the Lord be glorified by our lives, for we have no other purpose than just that! He will do this through this experience! We have praised him in the public eye, and we have acknowledged to this city that we are the servants of the living God. We remain pure of heart and contrite of spirit. We *are his righteous children by the blood of Jesus.* He *will* deliver all of this into our hands and be greatly glorified.

You know what is really wild? After the last few years of walking with the Lord at these increased levels of relationship, I actually say these words and *believe* them. So many times the Lord has had to meet me in the midst of my doubt, but not this time. On this matter, I'm all the way there.

One last thing. The outpouring of public support has been immense. Lori and I both have been flooded with calls and cards of support (Lori has gotten a ton of flowers). A week ago we recorded the program Flashpoint. As we were walking out of the station, the receptionist came out from behind the desk and asked if she could have a hug from Lori! Then she complimented me for standing beside my wife. It has been like that continually. The Lord our God is exalting us before the people even in the midst of this trial. It just so fascinates me that what the Enemy means for evil, the Lord will use to glorify himself. So many times I have been moved to tears with friendly calls, useful advice, and positive comments from others.

Here's a note of spiritual irony. Years ago (probably 1984), when working for my stepfather, Eddie, we had a court judgment obtained against us unfairly. While driving back in the midst of my stress, I suddenly started praising and thanking God for the adversity! The judgment was ultimately reversed. The other day I had asked John Jacobsen [my first assistant] to follow up on a lawyer's references as I was considering hiring her. The district judge he called in the county in which this lawyer practiced told John to be sure and tell me that he was praying for me. How very kind. But the interesting part is that this was the judge who in 1984 levied a judgment against us and that I learned the importance of thanking the Lord for adversity in my life. God is good. I am so grateful.

Don't get me wrong. I am confident Lori would never *volunteer* to go through this ordeal again. But in hindsight, the closing of her medical practice and the removal of her license also stripped away the people pleasing spirit that had afflicted her all of her life. Ever since she was a small child, Lori desperately worked to make everything and everyone around her happy, allowing it to somehow feed her sense of self-worth. Her addiction experience and humiliation forced her to look only at pleasing God and nobody else—including her husband. It was impossible to please everybody because, in the end, people are unpredictable and untrustworthy in their affection. Seeking acceptance from others proved to be an empty, unpredictable pursuit at best. Like silver going through the proverbial furnace, the entire experience stripped the "I must be perfect" dross from her life. It was something akin to what I had to go through in the mid 1980s. I could not muscle my way into being happy. Neither could she.

As stated in my journal entry, there was a deeply moving outpour of support as well. It seemed that everywhere I went (Lori was out of state for several months at a treatment center in the spring of 2002)—restaurants, even elevators—perfect strangers would come up to me and say "We're praying for you and your wife." It moves me even to write this memory. It happened literally *scores* of times. Finally, it dawned on me that God was raising up intercessors on our behalf! People were praying by the drove for us! Praying for us? It was a profound realization (and a continuing experience throughout my tenure for which we will always be deeply grateful). But something else was slowly dawning on me as stranger after stranger approached me. A community was actually watching us to see how this so-called "Christian" couple was going to walk out this period of public adversity. In a way, like it or not, we had become something like poster children for the Christian community. Would all the pressure tear us apart? Would we fall on our faces? There were those that hoped we would. After all, it was not only great theater, but I was also learning quickly that not everyone was exactly thrilled at my appointment as district attorney.

So when did "joy" finally show up? It was a gradual process and a time of continuing prayer. We kept petitioning God and reminding him of his promises. There were times when Lori felt like a total failure and Satan would torment her miserably and unmercifully. This spiritual warfare required great effort, not unlike what took place in our bedroom that Christmas. It was as if the Devil was losing his grip on territory over which he had once held firm control—Lori's self-esteem—and he was putting up a last desperate struggle. Finally, early in the summer of 2006, I remember Lori turning to me and making a statement I once thought I might never hear. She said, "I've never felt this good in my entire life." It was a remarkable moment. She had been soaking up God's promises and finally fully embraced the truth that she did not have to be a medical doctor to please God. He loved her for herself. She need please no one else. To paraphrase a martyred missionary, Jim Elliot, "It took losing something I could not keep in order to gain something I could not lose." Lori lost some things, but the gain was a longtime prayer being answered and God's gift of joy revealed.

It has been my observation and experience that shedding doubt is something like peeling layers off an onion. Sometimes we are only able to shed one thin layer at a time. Sometimes an experience will take quite a hunk out of our onion of doubt. Without doubt, one attribute of God I have observed is that, upon invitation, he will get aggressively engaged in increasing our faith (which, of course, is the shedding of doubt). This is not to say that he wouldn't do it on his own without our specific request, but I'm not sure God is very moved by our disinterested complacency. I look back at this chapter's tumultuous and painful events and I see an amazingly loving, faithful Father, and a much, much smaller onion.

God wants to increase and augment the atmosphere of faith in which we live. This very atmosphere is death to the areas of life holding us back from God's best—areas of low self-esteem, pride, discouragement, addiction, or whatever else is the ball and chain around the heart. As I reflect on God's loved ones in the Bible and how he never forsook them through their circumstances, I see that same great consistency in the way he was with Lori and me through our very public and private adversity. He heard our prayers and saw our faith, not as it was but as it would become. God will get aggressively engaged in increasing one's faith. The only requirement is that we ask. This is the atmosphere, the life, he has for all.

CHAPTER EIGHT

A TRIP TO THE AMERICAN WITCH DOCTOR

The depth of our relationships has always been defined by our willingness to communicate with one another. We never truly fall in love without first having a conversation. We never stay in love without keeping the conversation going. The atmosphere of faith is also about a relationship, a relationship that depends on a conversation known as "prayer."

It seems to me that in American Christianity we often approach prayer like we do the fast food restaurant window. Not only do we want our ordered up "prayer burger" now, but we want it *our* way. Immediate gratification or we move on. Many Christians lose heart because we come before the throne of God thinking we are at Burger King. As I reflect on this I am embarrassed at all the prayers I have *ceased* praying because I saw no response and I moved on. We stop praying, perhaps even on the cusp of victory, because of a cultural nuance. We are impatient Americans. Well, God is not an American, nor is he Chinese, but I suspect Christians in China, a country whose cultural patience is legendary, have a far easier time "waiting" on God than do many American Christians. As the apostle Paul said, we must not lose heart (Gal. 6:9). God is in the character building business and one of those traits he wishes to build is perseverance. As we build up our perseverance, we are building up our faith, and as we build up our faith, we are able to believe God for greater and greater things. Apart from the Lord's mercy, we cannot expect to see magnificent responses to prayer without increasingly strengthened faith. All of this simply takes time. He has quite a lot of it.

But I also suspect that even before the issue of perseverance rears its head, we have an even greater problem. Most of us just don't see the point of prayer in any event, because we wonder if we're not just talking into the air when we pray. I recall as a young teenager never taking prayer seriously. If one were to really dissect the root of my lack of seriousness, it was probably that I viewed prayer, and maybe even God, in something of the superstition category. For example, at the time I had very bad eyesight and wore thick glasses, and I was having a very difficult time getting contact lenses to work for me. I was desperate because I wanted to look cool and thick glasses were way *not* cool. I went to more than one optometrist trying to get a pair of contact lenses to wear with comfort (these were the old hard lens days). I think it might have been my dad who suggested we get his mother to pray for this as we all knew from family lore that *her* prayers got answered. We actually never paused to reflect on why *our* prayers *weren't*; we just went to "Mom" as we called my grandmother. In fact, I have no memory of us praying at all on the subject. Rather, like some primitive jungle tribe, we just took a trip to the witch doctor. In this case, it was Mom.

My grandmother's reputation for answered prayer was well earned. Dad once told me a story about grandmother "Mom" that occurred when he was a little boy. They were dirt poor living in Ft. Smith, Arkansas, and Mom would make what little money they had by sewing for the old "WPA" program instituted by President Roosevelt. Dad was the ninth of nine kids, and his father died when Dad was three. It was in the thirties during the depths of the Great Depression, when one night my father heard his mother weeping and went in to her bedroom to find out what was wrong. She told him they had no food in the house and did not know what she was going to feed the children in the morning. She was on her knees beside the bed praying to God for food. Dad never forgot the knock on the front door early the next morning and someone dropping off a bucket of flour and milk solely in response to his mother's prayer. He said it was not the only time that sort of thing happened between his mother and God.

When we went to Mom, she happily agreed to pray that I would be able to wear contact lenses. Sure enough, the very next time we went to the optometrist the lenses worked. *Oooh!* I thought, *that was down-right spooky.* Those prayers of Mom sure work! I was happy, got my wish filled and gave God not another thought. I never did the math on what was it about Mom that moved God to answer her prayers as opposed to other folks. It never dawned on me that she and God might have actually had quite a relationship going. Mom and God knew each other quite well. Mom really liked God and God apparently really liked Mom. It was well known in the family that the heavenly Father seemed to enjoy helping Mom out for some reason. Now, in retrospect, I can easily see that Mom "hung out" with God in prayer. She very much wanted us to "go deep" (as she put it) in our relationship with God. But I just never put two and two together at the time. If I called upon God it was not because I liked him or wanted to get chummy with him; it was because I *wanted* something and I wanted it right then. And I wanted it my way. If I couldn't get it myself, I would go through Mom. I figured that even though God knew what I was up to, he still liked Mom so much that he would answer *her* prayer for me.

As I get to know God better, I am increasingly realizing that Mom didn't have anything going with God that the rest of us couldn't have as well. She walked in an atmosphere of faith. As I get to know my heavenly Dad better and better, I grow in my understanding of who he is, and what he likes and doesn't like. It was the same thing in getting to know my earthly father. Let me repeat that it was the same thing in getting to know my earthly father. Knowing we are made in God's image (according to Genesis 1:27) removes a lot of the mystique relationally with God. As parents we love to be adored and revered by our children. So does God. Our parents respond accordingly. So does God. Therefore, since I have a brain and I have been pursuing the heck out of my heavenly Dad for quite a while now, and realizing this is not rocket science, guess what? I *know* that Dad *really, really* likes me. Seriously, I am probably one of his absolute, most favorite kids in the whole wide world! Of course, I suspect I have several million siblings around the world today who claim *they* are his favorites, but I say, "No Way! Surely it's me!" Can't you imagine a few million of God's little kids vying for a piece of the Divine Lap? God loves us all, but he must get a kick out of the ones who are just crazy about him. Wouldn't you? The thing is, when we extravagantly love our heavenly Dad, he extravagantly loves us right back. My grandmother was unique, but only in the sense that so comparatively few of God's children love him as madly as she did and take advantage of the rich relationship he makes available.

We shouldn't make this more complicated than it is. Many people figure that since their parents were jerks and made them jump through hoops for attention, then surely the Father in heaven must operate in the same way. It's like mistrusting the reflection of a perfect mirror just because ours has always been broken. Some Christians turn a relationship into a religious exercise. I suppose this happens because when something fabulous is freely available, we figure there must be a catch somewhere.

Our heavenly Dad knows when we have been willing to pursue him, even when we wondered if we were talking into the air, even when we were full of doubt, even when we were hearing *nothing,* and even when we were sincerely frightened. We *decided* to search for him with all our hearts. We chose to walk in an atmosphere of faith even when there was no immediate gratification. This is why God was nuts about my grandmother. She was not content for a shallow relationship. Rather, she wanted to "go deep," and the heavenly Father honored her effort.

God has always loved us, and like us he loves to be pursued. This separates those seriously in love with God from the "not so much." His *promise* is to respond to our pursuit. That has been my experience, and even if the response takes years, he does respond. God *wants* to be pursued, he *wants* to be found, and he *wants* to *answer* believing prayer.

> Then you will call upon Me and come and pray to Me, and I will listen to you. And you will seek Me and find Me when you search for Me with all your heart.
>
> —Jeremiah 29:11–12

God has something special for each of us.

CHAPTER NINE

THE HEADWINDS OF RESPONSIBILITY
(STATE OF OKLAHOMA V. TERRY LYNN NICHOLS)

In the atmosphere of faith, there are times we don't even realize God was present until afterwards, when we notice that single trail of footprints left in the sand as he carried us through our experience.

"This community has been deeply and sharply divided upon the appropriate course of action to take in this case. Those who know me know that I govern my life with a set of core principles that guide me in my personal decision-making. It is my reliance upon these core principles that helps me stay the course and do what I believe to be the right thing versus what might be an easier course of action under given circumstances . . . It is my best judgment at this time that the course of action I now take is one acting in the best interests of this community. I will not waiver in performing what I believe to be my duty to the citizens of this county. Even at the expense of my personal popularity."
—Wes Lane public statement of September 5, 2001, announcing his decision to continue with the prosecution of the Terry Lynn Nichols case

It was a pleasant April 19 morning in 1995 when I arrived at my wife's medical office. I had just come from the annual Metro Prayer breakfast in downtown Oklahoma City. I was on a leave of absence from the district attorney's office. My grandfather, R.O. Burbridge, had passed away a few months before, and the small Christian foundation bearing his name, The Burbridge Foundation, was in disarray. "Gran," as we called him, was something of a wealthy eccentric, reveling in buying his clothes at thrift shops and driving a dilapidated old Ford Maverick. He was a successful business entrepreneur but was, like the car he drove, a maverick himself. Always something of an unpredictable mystery to most of us, in his elderly state he handled the records and business of the foundation in a mysterious way as well. As a family, we were now scrambling, trying to put the pieces together to satisfy the various governmental interests, like the IRS, as well as to figure out what direction to take the foundation now that its founder was gone. My mother, the new president, had her hands very full, and I took a few months off to help the family.

Upon entering Lori's office, instead of the usual hustle-bustle taking place of patients coming and going, everyone was gathered around a small television set. The screen was filled with a downtown panorama, black smoke billowing against a lazy blue sky. The television commentators were filling the air time speculating over what might have happened. At that early moment, the guess was that there had been a gas line explosion of some sort. Something that must have taken place only minutes after I collected my car and left the downtown area. The blast occurred at 9:02 A.M. A call went out over the air waves for medical personnel to come and help and Lori quickly ordered her patient schedule cancelled before going downtown. She would arrive to a very tragic scene. A couple and their two small daughters had been standing in line in one of the government offices when the building blew. The floor split apart between the two little girls and one was now dead. Lori sewed up their distraught mother's face, describing the injury as being like "a bread knife had sliced her head leaving cheek and ear dangling." The father had also sustained internal injuries requiring surgery as well.

Like millions of others, a television screen was my introduction to the Alfred P. Murrah Federal Building domestic terrorist bombing. I had, of course, no idea that morning I would ultimately have a role to play in the matter.

As the truth of the blast's origin began to unfold, all we as citizens of Oklahoma City could do was to try and get our heads around the shocking realization that a grievous and unfathomable act of mass murder had taken place. Despite the fact that I was well acquainted with the evil I observed as a prosecutor, I could not fathom a heart doing such a massive act of violence against innocents. One hundred and sixty eight men, women, and children lay dead beneath the rubble, not to mention the three unborn children still in the wombs of three of the deceased. Over eight hundred others were injured.

And so we grieved in our various ways. I was acquainted with a few of those killed in the blast. My stint as a drug prosecutor had taken me on occasion over to the Drug Enforcement Administration office housed on an upper floor of the Murrah building. But unlike others, I had lost no loved ones; no one close and dear to my heart. I could not begin to grasp what others must have been feeling at that time. And yet, there was the strangest sense of collective grief. Like most others in Oklahoma City, for the first couple of days after the blast I went about in shock. Then, on the third day, I found myself at home for lunch.

It had become cool and rainy out, and I fixed myself a bowl of soup. Suddenly, as I leaned over the bowl in the silence of my kitchen, I felt a familiar thickness in my throat and constriction in my chest. With little warning, tears started their slow trek out of the corners of my eyes. This was unexpected, and I have no idea what triggered it. All I could do was put down my spoon and give into the release of the pent up emotion that had been building for days. It was my first small grasp of the fact that we were, in some way, all victims. An entire city had been assaulted when a Ryder rental truck bomb containing approximately five thousand pounds of ammonium nitrate fertilizer, nitromethane, and diesel fuel was detonated in front of the Murrah Building destroying the building and damaging many buildings located nearby.

Timothy McVeigh claimed to have specifically arranged the explosives for maximum killing. It was the largest terrorist attack on American

soil in history before the September 11, 2001 attacks in New York City.
McVeigh would later be found guilty of the attack and be sentenced
to death.

Six years and a couple of months later, I found myself sworn in as the
Oklahoma County District Attorney. At that time Terry Nichols, an ac-
complice of Timothy McVeigh in the bombing of the federal building,
was sitting in solitary confinement in the Oklahoma County Jail. Prior
to my appointment as DA, I was an assistant district attorney under
Bob Macy. I ran the juvenile division as its director for six years. In
this country, the average prosecutor's office is comprised of fewer than
five lawyers. Oklahoma County had ten times that, typically having on
staff fifty lawyers, with a support staff of one hundred. The size of our
population, around six hundred thousand, ranked us in the seventy-five
largest metropolitan jurisdictions. At the time we filed roughly eight
thousand felony, fifteen thousand misdemeanor, twenty five hundred
delinquent, and five hundred child welfare cases every year. We were a
very busy office. That has never changed. My division, located several
miles away from the main downtown offices, dealt with those last three
thousand cases of a delinquent and child welfare nature.

Away from the downtown hub of prosecutorial activity, it was not
hard to get completely out of the loop in the discussions surrounding prosecuting Nichols, or anything else for that matter. Other than
"water cooler" conversations that everyone else across the metropolitan
area was having, I had no substantive discussions with either victims or
law enforcement concerning the issues or merits of a state prosecution.
Other than closely following the federal prosecution of McVeigh and
Nichols, I was largely in the dark, like any other citizen. I knew that my
boss, like most of us, was frustrated that Nichols had slipped the death
penalty noose at the federal level. That, in the opinion of everyone I
knew both in and out of the office, had been a travesty of justice. To no
surprise of those working for him, Bob Macy planned to rectify that.

From my limited assistant's perspective, I knew our office was overwhelmed by murder cases. We always had more than we could easily
handle, especially considering that like most state prosecutor's offices it
was very difficult to maintain experienced legal talent. Young, promis-
ing lawyers with big student loans get married, start having kids, and

pretty soon it gets tough to make ends meet on a prosecutor's salary. Many are forced to leave for the greener financial pastures of private practice. Murder cases particularly demand experienced legal talent, and we were having a rough time keeping experienced lawyers on staff. Two of our most experienced homicide prosecutors were assigned to the Nichols case. I figured it would be a full time job for both of them, considering the voluminous amount of work to be done pasting together a circumstantial evidence case with thousands of bits of evidence. I had done that sort of work on a much smaller but no less complicated scale in some other cases. I was wondering how our office could handle the regular caseload demand and add the massive Nichols case on top of everything else. And hadn't he already had a trial? I couldn't help but wonder about all those other murder victim family members who had not even had so much as a preliminary hearing in their own long trek for justice.

A Honeymoon gone Missing

My introduction to dealing with the media took place in the "Blue Room" at the State Capitol. The occasion was the governor's press conference announcing my appointment as DA. It had been a heady few days since the night Governor Frank Keating called me at home to tell me he was appointing me to fill the unexpired term of my retiring boss. It was a dream—and a fervent prayer—come true. And now, on June 12, 2001, I was to embark on an evolving journey towards a deep understanding of the old adage "be careful what you pray for." I would not officially become the district attorney until July first, but Governor Keating introduced me to the public via the press conference. I followed his announcement with some prepared words of my own, but the question on everybody's mind was the Nichols case. It would be my first opportunity to put my foot in my newly-very-public-mouth as one of the reporters asked what I would say to those victims who clamored for a state trial.

"I think there are a ton of victims in this case who are of a different opinion on that. There will be some changes," I ineptly commented. This off-the-cuff and uninformed remark would send a chilling shockwave amongst those supportive of the trial, both outside and inside our own office. It publicly exposed the fact that I had severe doubts about whether to proceed. In fact, from my point of view, someone was going to need to convince me why I shouldn't just dismiss the case and move on.

Bob Macy must have started sweating bullets once I made the public slip. My former fellow prosecutors, and now my employees, weren't entirely sure how to deal with me on the subject either, since our official relationship had now shifted.

One of the very reasons Macy retired was the stress over the Nichols case. This case permeated all of the other stresses the job carried, the entirety of which was physically killing him. Yet, despite receiving so much public assault and even early federal governmental opposition to get the case filed and Terry Nichols brought to Oklahoma, he didn't twist my arm. He was probably just as surprised as anyone else to learn I was not an automatic "true believer" over the prosecution, especially since I was one of the three assistants he recommended to Governor Keating as his replacement. Knowing my old boss well, I suspect he had a couple of moments thinking some pretty salty thoughts about his independent former employee; however, he was kind enough not to share them with me.

The truth was I just did not have enough information, and I was certainly learning that the Nichols prosecution did not seem to be a popular decision on Macy's part. Whether I wanted it or not, I was catching the opinion of seemingly everyone I bumped into. As I told the press on the date of my swearing-in, "Let's face it, I am going to make half the world glad and half the world mad. I want to know in my heart of hearts I am doing the right thing."

The complaint I heard the most—and the complaint that ultimately became the most irritating to me—was about the money . . . the money . . . the money. It didn't bother me at first. Maybe not even the first fifty times I heard it. But the money refrain ultimately became like fingernails on a chalkboard to my ears. Even though I was leaning heavily against the prosecution, there was a simple explanation for my irritation over the money subject, a reason driven into me over many years of holding sobbing crime victims. Loved ones of dead victims don't care about money. For that matter, juries don't either. Neither of them wants to hear from the government that something important for justice was not done, or that could have been done, because it cost too much money. *I'm sorry Mrs. Smith, we could positively identify your daughter's killer with a DNA test, but we don't want to spend the money—which, by the way, we do have and, by the way, is the sort of thing the money we are given is for.* People want to believe their dead child is worth whatever it costs to achieve justice. In their view, that is the government's job and that is why they pay their taxes. And in truth, they are right.

So, despite my personal opinion about a retrial, the money chant grated against my career as a victim's advocate in the justice system. What especially got frustrating was the fact that "taxpayer" dollars were not even the source of funding we were using. The expenses would come from the court fund which is made up of fees and fines paid by individuals and defendants using the court system. In other words, the system funded itself. Whereas my budget did come from taxpayer dollars, if I chose to continue the case, I was determined to do so out of my existing budget and not ask the legislature for help. Had I asked, I felt confident they would not have helped anyway, given public sentiment. Ultimately, the money complaints almost became counterproductive as they only steeled my resolve not to have my decision based upon the contrary and whimsical wind of my own political self-interest.

But to complicate matters, I suspected there was something deeper lurking in the hearts of many of these trial opponents, a hidden objection that was not being expressed. They might say it was the money but deep down, at least with some of them, I believe they feared a retrial of Terry Nichols would pull a scab off the heart of an entire community. We were all wounded. We were all trying to heal. We all grieved in our different ways and were trying to get past the moment and move on with our lives. I could understand that reason because it was from the heart.

Opinions were coming at me from every direction, including those that had my supposed best political interest in mind. These opinions might come from my real friends, or from people pretending to be my friends—the latter category being individuals who once upon a time never cared whether they were *my* friend at all but now wanted to be "the DA's" friend. But even most of them were still well meaning. They

105

weren't thinking about the proverbial big picture of the case other than how it would impact my own political big picture. I never knew how to tell them how actually offensive that argument was to me. So I would patiently listen, not pursuing the line of thought, changing the subject as I could. Still, from their point of view, this case was a "political tar baby," as someone put it, that I needed to dump and dump quickly.

So, instead of the typical honeymoon-like grace period that "newbies" get in public office, all I had to do was enter a restaurant or other public place and have people come up to me and complain about my prosecuting the Nichols case. My public life would start off with a storm, and in some ways, would never cease. The storm over Nichols would especially continue through the following campaign summer of 2002. My political opponent of the time was hitting the airwaves announcing he would flat out drop the Nichols case if elected. His television commercials always showed him alongside his supporter, the popular former mayor of Oklahoma City, the mayor during the time of the bombing no less. My volunteers making campaign phone calls would often meet with an earful of complaints surrounding the continued prosecution of Nichols, which, at times, produced panic amongst my campaign staff. And the drum beat of the incessant media polls showed that most people wanted to drop the matter and just move on.

And, at least for a couple of months at the start of my tenure that hot summer of 2001, I was with them.

Promises, Promises

A prosecutor learns a hard lesson in his career when he fails to discuss his case with the crime victim. Or, in the case of a murder, with the deceased's love ones. Macy drilled that into us, as he and every other DA should. One of the worst infractions a prosecutor can commit is to negotiate and plead out a case without having discussed it with the victim of the crime, and the worst of the worst offenses is when the crime is murder.

I entered into my first weeks as district attorney with the belief that the families of the bombing victims were clamoring for a state trial for the primary reason that they wanted to achieve the death penalty that eluded Nichols in the first case. I never met with any of them up to this point, but that is what I assumed from the scuttlebutt.

I have always been an advocate of the death penalty. I had tried death penalty murder cases, and during my career I even had murderers I sent to death row executed. I even attended the execution of one particularly evil killer I had put away, but it was never something to which I took a liking. It was business, not a notch on my prosecutorial gun. You murder someone and if it fits the lawful circumstances, you, the killer, put your own life at severe risk.

The first duty of government is to protect the public, and violent crime to me was a form of warfare. I knew that messages were sent to the criminal community with the death penalty, something death penalty opponents deride. But in Oklahoma County we knew of instances where decisions to murder store clerks were at times made based upon what county the potential killer was standing in at the time he contemplated pulling that trigger. In one noted instance years earlier, a murderer had killed a store clerk during a robbery and during his videotaped confession, learned to his great shock and chagrin that he had committed the crime in Oklahoma County—he thought he had been in neighboring Cleveland County. His exasperated comment upon learning the truth was: "Oh my God, Macy is going to fry my a—!"

Criminals on the street know the reputation of their local district attorney's office, and while taking steps in our office to make sure the system was regarded as fair and just, I fully intended to maintain our tough reputation on the street. Fear has always been a useful tool in protecting the public, whether in crime prevention or with the mutually assured destruction of nuclear weaponry. It's simple human nature.

But I was troubled in late July, 2001, as I walked into the Oklahoma City Police Training Center to meet with the scores of family members impacted by the deaths of their loved ones in the Murrah Building. Nichols had already had one shot at the death penalty, and I did not want to be a party to simple blood lust. As I said earlier, I was deeply concerned about our ability to handle Nichols in light of the backlog of murder cases we already carried. Why did these people want a second trial?

It was at that meeting when everything began to change for me. In many ways it was not dissimilar to the meetings I had had with family members in other cases. Only this was bigger. Some brought photographs of their loved one with them, wanting desperately for me to put a face on a live human being, not just a gruesome crime scene or autopsy picture. I listened to them tell of that special person, of his or her plans and dreams, dreams that were now cold and empty and gone forever, dreams forever stolen by a senseless act of bloody violence. It is always especially hard when the victim is a child, and there were so very many dead children in this case. Small lives with no opportunity to ever know what it would be like to grow up, to fall in love, to have their own family. Little lives cut short without ever tasting life and what it was meant to be.

But I was prepared for that; indeed, I was steeled for it. All I had to do was keep focused on other little children, other lives with their own dreams cut short, lives from other cases that were looking to us who had never had a trial before. But then I started hearing something I had not expected, something for which I was not prepared. It was something I already understood technically as a lawyer but that I had not absorbed into my heart. As these often intense, emotionally charged individuals poured their hearts out to me, I began to slowly *feel* a deep realization that would ultimately change the entire equation for me: *These families were still waiting for justice*, for in their view they had never had a trial at all! I was dumbfounded. I was not witnessing a blood thirsty mob; I was witnessing a group of people crying out for someone to take responsibility for the life of their loved one. Although I well knew the federal trial of Nichols and McVeigh had been centered upon the eight federal agents killed in the blast, these people were sincerely hurting that the trial had not been, in their opinion, about the lives of the one hundred and sixty others. One hundred and sixty three, counting the children who died in the womb. As one person put it, "Nobody has ever been tried for the death of my child!"

I scheduled two meetings at different times in order to accommodate as many families as could come. The tone from both meetings was the same. Whereas there were some that did not advocate for another trial, I could not shake off what I had absorbed as I went home to my own intact family that night, deeply moved and stirred to my core. So many citizens were clamoring for me to simply dismiss the case, but scores of hurting people were looking for me to stand up for them to carry out a promise made by my predecessor. A promise made by their government to seek justice. These people were actually looking *to me*, and the weight of it all bore down upon my shoulders more deeply than ever.

At one point in one of the two meetings, I was asked point blank if I thought I had an obligation to keep Bob Macy's promise. I said, "No," but it rang hollow within me even as the word left my lips. On one hand I couldn't be expected to keep every promise made by any DA before me. That wasn't reasonable. Yet it was becoming clear that what they were asking me to do was not unreasonable. It was all about responsibility—responsibility of a man who had technically never been held responsible for these many deaths, and my own sworn responsibility as this community's minister of justice and chief law enforcement officer. I knew then that I could not just simply dismiss the case, however much easier it would have made my life. Terry Nichols had to be made to take responsibility. It was a shift of position that would cost three difficult years and much political capital to bring to fruition.

And so that summer, it became incumbent upon me to do what prosecutors always do, which is to meet with a defendant's attorney about their case. I had given ear to everybody else, now it would be Nichols' turn. Nichols' first hope was that I would outright dismiss the case. In an early telephone conversation prior to meeting, his lawyer went down the list of all the reasons why this case was such a burden to the community and should be jettisoned—the two primary reasons being the community suffering and, of course, the money. By this time, however, I had mentally eliminated the option of straight out dismissal and was more focused on what Terry Nichols was willing to do, rather than what I was.

Plea bargains have always been an unsavory aroma to the public nostrils. Yet the reality is that without them, the justice system would quickly grind to a screeching halt. It is completely impossible to have a jury trial for each of the millions of cases filed every year nationally. There are simply not enough judges and lawyers to do it all. Yet, it is the stuff of which political campaigns are made. The political opponent claims he or she would never have made such a "deal" if *they* had been DA, and the very word "deal" is spit out with a look of twisted disgust as if they were trying to expurgate an unexpectedly sour piece of candy. The public in turn raises a wary eyebrow at the very thought that somewhere lawyers are somehow making distasteful agreements that doubtlessly circumvents justice. Television reporters in their allotted news minute report on a case and how the DA gave a defendant a reduced sentence. The camera focuses on us and we get about eight seconds to explain what might have taken weeks and months to work out. Cases can be extremely complicated depending upon what we think we can prove and choices often boil down to getting a conviction on someone with less of a penalty than what we might like in order to get something at all.

On more than one occasion, I conducted staff meetings with my prosecutors warning that the public's perception of justice would often depend upon how they were able to respond to a television camera in the sound bite allotted them. The concept of "justice" can be a slippery slope, and several times throughout my tenure we were faced with a news reporter more motivated by what was shocking on its face than in presenting the deeper truths of why we might have had to do what we did in a particular case. The news story presents the face of a weeping victim complaining about how we were irresponsibly lenient to a criminal when the whole truth was that there was no way we would have won at trial and that criminal would have gone free had we not done what we did. Just because the case looks good in print, does not mean a judge would have allowed a jury to hear the juicy bit of information appearing in the paper. The sad truth is that the public's perception of justice may have no connection to the reality of justice coming from a prosecutor's office. It is a constant state of tension in any office, and so it was in mine.

In Nichols, however, such realities were somewhat turned on their ear as the public largely believed justice was *already* done. I doubt seriously that the public's perception of justice would have suffered had I simply dismissed the case. It would certainly have avoided another three years of public battle. On the other hand, after the victim meetings I realized I could not and would not do that, which then gave rise to my next dilemma.

It boiled down to this: I had a death penalty case pending for an alleged mass murderer. How could I agree to plea this magnitude of murderer when I wouldn't plea another defendant for even a single murder? The simple answer is you don't. But it stopped being a simple answer after the two community exhausting federal trials in Denver. An Oklahoma trial would actually be the *third* time Oklahoma City would have to relive the bombing in its entire gory splendor since the previous separate trials for McVeigh and Nichols.

The only principled reason I could even begin to associate with an agreement to *not* pursue the death penalty for Nichols was what I believed to be the reality of the community suffering that would take place with such a spectacle. It was not a figment of my imagination that the sort of "piling on" re-victimization of thousands and thousands of individuals would take place as they were forced to yet again relive the horror of that event of massive death and destruction via a public trial. It was a very harsh reality spelled out clearly with the degree of community angst pouring out from every direction. That immense anguish was not lost on me as I prepared to enter into discussions with Nichols' attorney, although I was still deeply uncomfortable even with that sort of reasoning. It was something of a small comfort that I believed the victim families were focused on Nichols' accountability and less so on his head.

All these internal moral dilemmas I was laboriously working through turned out to be something of a wasted exercise because the matter would largely resolve itself by the end of August, 2001. It took only about one meeting in my office with Nichols' attorney to come to the jaw dropping realization that Terry Nichols did not want to take responsibility for murder. At that point I could see why it was that the lawyer was trying so hard to get me to dismiss the case outright without ever getting to an informal discussion of pleading the case. Nichols did not see himself as having committed murder! I remember sitting there in something approaching stunned disbelief. Was I even hearing this correctly? Did this guy really just tell me that his client was only willing to consider pleading to charges of *involuntary* manslaughter, charges that were tantamount to claiming he didn't mean to kill anyone? In my mind, the charge of involuntary manslaughter was something more appropriate to someone driving recklessly down the highway and inadvertently killing a pedestrian.

The evidence was overwhelming about Nichols' diligent efforts to help Timothy McVeigh achieve a stupendous explosion. But I knew why Nichols was making this suggestion, as although his federal jury had convicted him of conspiracy with McVeigh, they had not convicted him of murder, finding him guilty of involuntary manslaughter instead. It was for this reason he had avoided the death penalty.

It was a telling moment there in my office that summer day. Outside my office window a significant piece of the public was hoping to be relieved of this killer's burden. The Sheriff didn't even want the man in his jail! But now I was getting a bit of insight of which the public was unaware. Terry Nichols had been proclaiming himself to be a Christian since his arrest, a new convert. I had just received a telling insight into his so-called "Christian" heart. It was to impact my view of the case, but not in the way Nichols likely hoped.

Two Different Crimes, Two Very Different Men

Some fifteen years earlier, when I finally made that real commitment to follow Christ, I had occasion to read the autobiography of Chuck Colson entitled *Born Again*.[1] Colson had been President Richard Nixon's legal counsel in the White House and one of the president's closest confidantes. It was the unbelievable pressure of an unraveling presidency and the attendant Watergate era investigations that finally overwhelmed and compelled Colson to become a Christian. I will never forget my amazement as I read the account of how he responded to the federal indictments against him. As he tried to walk the twin paths of criminal defendant and fledgling Christian disciple, he discovered that he had to make a choice; he could not live with one foot in both worlds. On one path he was constantly struggling with all the legal maneuvering necessary to try and save himself from prison. On the other path, he wanted no closet skeletons, just freedom to speak his newfound Truth without people wondering whether this faith was real or just a sham. He made reference to this paradox with a quote of Dietrich Bonhoeffer from his book *The Cost of Discipleship*:

The first step which follows Christ's call cuts the disciple off from his previous existence. The call to follow at once produces a new situation. To stay in the old situation makes discipleship impossible.[2]

Colson ultimately realized that the path to freedom in Christ would mean the loss of his freedom from prison. There could be no compromise. The old Chuck Colson's "world" wanted him to play the game. To be the new Chuck Colson required a clean break with the past, and it was a price he was willing to pay.

Colson shocked his lawyer by telling him he was going to plead guilty, and that he wanted no plea bargaining, no maneuvering, and no attempt to wrench something from the prosecution in return for lenience. He was going to take responsibility, to speak the truth of his involvement, to testify freely, to play a role in a nation's healing. He would set a very public example of what the character of new man in Christ was supposed to look like. He would send no mixed messages. Despite his lawyer's insistence that he believed they could win the case and make Colson a free man, Colson said no. He went to prison rather than disrespect his God.

I was deeply impacted by that. Colson was a role model to me as well. This was clearly a man after God's own heart. Here was a fledgling Christian who already understood the importance of the responsibility associated with his faith. It was my knowledge of a man's man like Colson stepping up to the plate like he did and pleading guilty from the start that stuck in my craw over the likes of Terry Nichols, the man who, according to his jailers, now spent the bulk of his time with his nose buried in a Bible. If ever there was a man who knew what he did, and if ever there was a man who should have wanted to repent and seek the forgiveness of both his God and the hundreds, even thousands, whom he had devastated, it was Terry Lynn Nichols.

I understood this also at an experiential level, which all the more disgusted me with what I viewed as a hypocritical position on Nichols' part. In the late 1980s, I felt compelled by my faith to go to a man I had wronged many years before. I had stolen from him when I was in college. It was clear to me that my faith demanded I deal with that. I knew I must go to the man, confess my deed and seek his forgiveness. He could have done whatever he wanted with me—tell my then boss Bob Macy, call the police, whatever. It did not matter for as I walked out my faith I could only come to the conclusion that it was simply inconsistent with that faith that I do anything less than take responsibility for my actions, even old ones. No blaming others or my circumstances. I needed to own what was mine and allow God to work his purposes out. I could not in good conscience claim to be a Christian without acknowledging there to be a code of conduct associated with that faith.[3]

I told Nichols' attorney that such an agreement was completely unacceptable and the only basis upon which we could even *begin* to have a formal discussion of a *possible* plea without the death penalty attached required his client having a change of heart and accepting responsibility for mass murder. Apart from that, proceeding along with the death penalty prosecution was inevitable.

Nichols refused.

On September 5, 2001, two months after taking office, I held what turned out to be a nationally televised press conference beneath what had become known as the "Survivor Tree." This eighty year old American elm stood on the grounds of what had been a parking lot across the street to the north of the Murrah Building. The entirety of the area was by that time a national memorial, and the tree a recognized symbol. The circular terrace surrounding the tree was crammed with people and cameras. I told very few people what I was going to announce that morning. The tension in the crowd of both victims and the curious was palpable. It was still difficult for me to comprehend that something with which I was involved had actually incurred national attention.

I announced my intent to continue with the state prosecution. As I spoke to the crowd, outlining the various concerns I had from the beginning and what I had determined concerning them, my view overlooked 168 empty chairs representing the dead.

A Relentless Wind

As the months continued, the pressure did not abate. It seemed we were plagued with one delay after another. The case kept getting continued for a variety of reasons. One preliminary hearing judge had already been removed from the case for inappropriate contact with the defense team. A second judge would quit the case on the very eve of what we thought would finally be the long sought after preliminary hearing. The state Supreme Court mysteriously held the case up for at least half a year on a relatively minor issue. The media faithfully reported the mounting defense expenses and all the delays and with every bump in the road it seemed another poll would be taken and another piece of the public would decide they now wanted it all to end.

I felt something of a brief reprieve after the contentious 2002 election was over and I was finally the "elected" DA as opposed to the "appointed." It had been an exhausting year and a half in office by the time the year rolled to an end. It seemed everything that could possibly rear its ugly head did so, not the least of which had been Lori's challenges with the prescription pain killer and her own set of criminal charges so very publicly aired. Even that would ultimately play its role in my view on prospective plea agreements with Terry Nichols.

By this time, the Nichols trial team consisted of several members, one of whom I found quite personable. He was a criminal law professor from another state, and he would call or come by from time to time to personably hammer on my resolve. The "team" knew that I had lost any sense of trust with Nichols' lead lawyer from various public ploys he pulled to jack up public pressure on me to dismiss the case. Even with the professor's efforts, there was an air of dissension on their legal team regarding the plea issue. Whereas they were by this time claiming Nichols was willing to plead to murder, small comments made me wonder if that was really true. I even wondered at times whether the lawyers might be split on whether they even wanted Nichols to plead.

The law professor was relentless, but I had reached a point in which I was much less inclined to be interested in dealing with the thought of a plea. I had finally found my sea legs for the job, and after dealing with the collective adversities of the first eighteen months I was very tired of playing the game with the Nichols team, when Nichols himself remained an enigma. More importantly, and as I expressed to others, I found it difficult to do for a white mass murderer what I would not do for a black convenience store clerk killer. I had reached that ultimate decision on several occasions by this time, and this was settling into a clear distinction for me. How was it fundamentally fair for me to plead this case now considering my stand in other cases? I knew what it was like to look a crying, begging family member of a death penalty defendant in the eye and say no to her request to not pursue the death penalty on her brother. It was not a pleasant experience. Was I supposed to dismiss a bill of particulars (the legal document initiating a death penalty prosecution) only when it suited me, or when it wasn't fun anymore? The issue of consistency and fairness was the principle I kept finding myself chafing against every time the subject of plea arose.

I might have developed those "sea legs," but I was also realizing the true loneliness of leadership. There were so very few on my staff to whom I could really let down my hair, so to speak. I had learned that a ship's crew keeps one eye on the captain for the source of their own confidence. And even those few with whom I could confide had no frame of reference to truly comprehend just how lonely it really is at the top. It wasn't their fault, of course. I could never have done so for Bob Macy when he was DA, and I was one of his fifty assistants. I also had no concept of the pressure that is associated with such a public, controversial and confrontational position. I could be sympathetic, but that was about it.

A couple of years earlier, before I had the slightest idea that I would ever actually be the district attorney, I was told by a couple of prophetic pastors that the Lord was sending me into the "arena of politics and the law" and that the he was going to make me more and more and more dependent upon him. At the time I had no concept of just how real that dependence would become. Whereas I had been blessed with many friends and supporters, they could not provide the peace I was so desperately seeking.

Journal: Sunday, January 5, 2003

I was sworn in as the *elected* District Attorney for Oklahoma County last Thursday. It was honestly almost anti-climatic. There had been so much water under that bridge having served in the post for eighteen months and having endured what has to have been one of the toughest years of my life. I started to review 2002 and noted my last entry was back in September. It was interesting to note that many of the issues with which I was contending in my last entry have not changed. A good example is with the on-going, never ending (or starting) Nichols case. The state is undergoing severe budget shortfalls which include the judicial system (and this includes my office). I'm getting pressure from folks about how Nichols' attorney is making millions of dollars representing this guy, which is directly resulting in courthouse people having pay cuts and special judge positions not being filled. And here I am pursuing this case even though our last judge quit a couple of months ago and we haven't even had a preliminary hearing. It's impacted my sleep several nights this last week. We should have already had a trial by now for crying out loud! I feel so alone. I don't know who to really talk to about this. Was I right in rebuffing attempts last winter to strike a plea agreement (although there is a question regarding whether there could have been one in the first place, since the defense attorneys were certainly not united). But the point of all this is not to talk about the Nichols case but rather about how inadequate I feel. These matters require the wisdom of a Solomon!

In some respects it is all so perfectly clear. I ponder on some of David's psalms and how helpless and inadequate he felt at times. Don't you know he was frustrated with guys like Joab (I mean I bet there was only a limited range of things he could share with that guy) and really sought godly counselors? So who is mine? Who is that gray headed fellow oozing with wisdom that I can so easily turn to in order to know what the right thing to do is in a given complicated scenario? . . . I can only come to the conclusion (and I believe my spirit is in agreement with this) that my prayer life is wholly inadequate. *I* am feeling wholly inadequate because my *prayer life* is wholly inadequate! My morning prayer has been pretty abbreviated and Lord knows my night prayer in bed with Lori has been, for the most part, pretty much the same; hitting the highlights, a sort of rubber stamp praying.

I just looked up from my computer and noticed there is a book I've never looked at and I don't even know how I got it. It's entitled *Praying the Scriptures*.[4] I pulled it down and looked at the back page. A line from it as well as a line I casually opened to, started me weeping. The line on the back page is, "One of the most frustrating aspects of prayer is not being able to find the right words to express what *dwells deep within your heart.*" That hit me pretty hard. But then I opened it up to the first chapter and another line caught my eye: "Prayer is talking to the Father, not simply because we are confused or confounded, *but because we are lonesome for Him.*" That gripped me again as I read it. I have indeed felt so terribly alone.

I just finished taking some time to read the first couple of chapters in the book I mentioned above (*Praying the Scriptures*). Indeed, it was a balm for which I have been seeking. All my concerns and sense of isolation and anxiety stem entirely from my spirit's longing to spend time with the Lord in a more meaningful way. There were many pearls of godly truth in what little I reviewed, and following reading this portion, I got on my face before the Lord, trusting him and expecting his provision. I am at peace. What is absolutely vital is that I accept his invitation to call upon him (Jer. 33:3). I came before him with prayer and supplication and with thanksgiving, and the peace of the Lord, which knows no comprehension, washed away my fears. Blessed be the name of the Lord my God! Praise his holy name!

Someone once pointed out to me that we never get more of Jesus than we do upon our conversion. He's already *all* there from the get-go. A part of me was stressed because I thought God showing up in my circumstances was somehow dependent upon my performance. Like one of the prophets of Baal on Mount Carmel (1 Kings 18), I thought if I danced harder or cut myself more deeply God would show up. I was beginning to learn (and still am) that both the power and peace that comes from the Lord is directly tied to my level of intimacy with him, which is far different than my head knowledge or performance. I may be able to quote a book on marriage to my wife, but that doesn't mean we have intimacy. My head might be stuffed with Bible verses and I might read Scripture three times a day and watch Christian television all night, but that doesn't mean I am being still and knowing God is God (Ps. 46:10). If there was any personal good coming from the blustering headwinds of responsibility in leadership, it was that they were blowing me into a deeper place of intimacy with God; a place of resting in him. These winds forced me to realize it was only in my release of control of my circumstances that I found myself actually in control of my anxiety and loneliness. It was just very hard for me to get my head around the fact that the action step God wanted from *this* leader was for me to simply rest in him. How very like God to require the opposite of everyone else's expectations.

That winter of 2003, I engaged for the last time in meetings with the Nichols lead attorney in a sort of plea negotiations, albeit as a reluctant participant to say the least. The Chief Justice of the Oklahoma Supreme Court was understandably vexed over the amount of money this operation was costing and shared that vexation with me. The massive amount of money flowing annually from the Oklahoma County Court Fund was distributed to courthouses around the state, thus monies diverted to Nichols was of no small concern to him. He very tactfully hoped we could settle the case but certainly never *ordered* me to engage in negotiations. Nobody had the authority to do that. Still, he *was* the Chief Justice and patent obstinacy on my part was not the wisest course of action. He was a good man with a job to do, and I saw no point in adding him to my growing list of enemies on a variety of fronts. After all, in any death penalty case I was always willing to listen, painful as it might be, when there is nothing new being said.

One of the former would-be preliminary hearing judges, the one who had quit at the eleventh hour, costing us more time and money, volunteered his services to help us negotiate, although I suspected that to most "negotiation" actually meant, "Get the DA to cave in." I was a reluctant participant, but in good faith would listen yet again to what the Nichols team had to say. The meetings took place secretly at an Oklahoma City hotel.

Before the process went along very far, I realized I had learned something years earlier that at this point I needed to apply to Nichols. I kept getting this sense that, although I could sit and listen all day long, it was an utter waste of my time if Terry Nichols' "heart" wasn't in the right place. In other words, why continue this discussion if Terry Nichols was still in a state of denial? I knew how to smoke that out and told the judge and Nichols' attorney that I wasn't going to participate in this process any further unless I was able to satisfy myself that Nichols himself was proceeding in this in good faith as well. I knew there were many victims with unanswered questions and there would be value to getting some of them answered. Thus, I had my prosecution team put together a list of five questions for Terry Nichols' response. I knew from past experience that motivated criminal defendants were ready to spill their guts about their involvement and ready to accept responsibility for their deed and come clean. If Nichols wasn't prepared to spill his guts, there was no point in even meeting.

The five questions put to Nichols were as follows:

1. Were you present during the purchase of ammonium nitrate, nitromethane, barrels and where was each purchased?
2. How and where was the bomb constructed and who was present, to include ingredients, percentage of fertilizer to nitromethane, boosters, initiator, and where did the recipe come from?
3. Where did any extra explosives from the Martin Marietta Rock Quarry end up?
4. Who participated in planning and who knew of the plan to blow up the Murrah Building and what was their level of participation?
5. Who went to the Murrah Building to select it or studied plans of it to plan the bombing?

For the most part we already had partial answers to these questions. Terry Nichols' test for willingness to be cooperative would come as a result of the degree he was willing to both own up to what we knew and then fill in the missing blanks. For example, we already knew and could prove his involvement with purchasing materials for the bomb. In his answer, he admitted to this but provided some additional details, such as elaborating on the method used to build the bomb itself. He also denied knowledge of any one else's involvement other than himself and Timothy McVeigh, who he pointed to as the master planner of the whole affair. These admissions, of course, were ultimately at odds with his trial team's sham efforts to introduce evidence of *other* people as having been the bombing culprits. The old "anybody but me did it" defense. The jury would never learn of Nichols' secret answers pointing only to him and McVeigh.

But one of the biggest unanswered questions was question number three. Where did the extra explosives stolen from the quarry end up? Hundreds of blasting caps and other explosives had been stolen from the quarry and their whereabouts were still unaccounted for. It was that question that betrayed his true "heart" as far as I was concerned and ended the negotiations. His response was simple: "After the bombing, I took those blasting caps and, along with other items, wrapped them in plastic and put them in a place where they would not be found by anyone."

"Put them in a place where they would not be found?" The question was, "where are they?"

In my view this was playing a game that I had no further motivation to play. I was tired of it. I had dealt with far too many repentant criminals to dance around with this unrepentant man. Indeed, when federal agents again searched his home almost a year after our trial was completed, they found buried deep below the house's duct system the hundreds of blasting caps and other materials he did not wish to tell us about.

It was shortly before the state trial was slated to begin that the final and, to me, the most revealing statement of Nichols' character came to light. Despite the fact that a gag order was still in place ordering all parties to not speak publicly about the case, his team allowed, yet again, one of their legal motions to become public record. Routinely, their filings had been "under seal" in order that the press could not obtain a copy. On this and another instance, the intent was for public pressure to come to bear on me to relent and do for him what I would not do for lesser murderers. In their motion they stated:

> We need to make perfectly clear on the record that Mr. Nichols is willing—and has been willing—to enter a no contest plea to all counts in the pending information if the State would dismiss the bill of particulars and not seek the death penalty against him.

Nolo Contendre

Put simply, a nolo contendre or "no contest" plea is not an admission of guilt. It is simply a statement that a defendant will not contest the charges against him. As District Attorney I disliked them intensely because I saw them as a defendant's refusal to take responsibility for his actions. This, in my opinion, ran contrary to the whole point of the justice system which, in part, was to force criminal defendants to own up to their actions. It ran contrary to a victim's need to have a criminal be held accountable as well for the damage he had inflicted. To me, it allowed a victim to be re-victimized by his or her assailant's refusal to step up and take responsibility for the pain inflicted. When I took office I observed that my staff was too readily agreeing to this sort of plea. In their defense, I knew that the agreed sentence might still be tough, but it was the principle of the matter and I ended the practice. I made more than a few criminal defense attorneys unhappy with my new office policy that if a defendant wanted to plead "no contest," his lawyer had to see me personally to explain why his client should not have to say "I'm guilty." It was a rare day and an unusual circumstance in which I agreed to a no contest plea. And why would I let Terry Nichols do something I wouldn't even allow my own wife?

In that earlier nightmarish period during which Lori sustained the unrelenting media glare due to her former addiction to prescription pain killers, there came a point in which she had to appear before a judge for plea and sentencing. She had been charged with two felony counts of obtaining a controlled substance by misrepresentation. I went with Lori and her lawyer to court and it was in the judge's chambers that Lori's lawyer met with the district attorney from another county who was assigned to prosecute her case. I held Lori's hand while we stood with frayed nerves waiting to hear what the prosecutor would want in the case. Although we knew that around the state cases like this were met with probation, it was still unnerving. It was tough enough on her just having to go through the humiliation of being charged as a criminal, much less being made a public spectacle. The weight of shame she carried was unbelievable. It certainly made me more circumspect in my remaining years of the raw power carried by a prosecutor to destroy lives if that power was not exercised with great care and restraint.

The door of the judge's chambers opened and Lori's attorney came over and told her what the prosecutor wanted as part of an agreed plea. As I expected, it was probation amongst other things. But then the lawyer added that the prosecutor had agreed to a "no contest" plea. That was news to us and that prospect had never crossed our minds. Legally, it would have been the smart thing to do. I knew that in the predatory world of plaintiff's civil lawyers, there was at least one letter going around from a law firm trolling for prospective clients amongst Lori's past patients. These sharks were looking for opportunities to make money by suing her for medical malpractice. Pleading "no contest" meant that they would have a slightly more difficult time in sullying her reputation at trial because Lori would never have pled guilty to any felonious conduct.

But before Lori could even respond to her attorney, I piped up and said, "No!" In my knee jerk response I probably could have been a bit more sensitive to the fact that Lori, by that time, was so beaten up by the whole affair that she was just barely hanging on emotionally. I made another comment about how she had either done the act or not. Why pretend she did not with a nolo contendre plea? Her lawyer and I went back and forth, explaining to Lori what it all meant and the pros and cons. In the end, Lori declined the no contest offer, not because she didn't think it was fair to her (what with the civil trial sharks circling), but because of my insistence. Another price she would get to pay for the privilege of being the DA's wife. Even though I was all concerned with the public perception of justice in the matter, I'm not now sure how much it mattered. In the long run she would still be smeared with comments about the "special deal" she had supposedly received, and I don't think that would have changed had she been sent to prison for the crime.

In the aftermath of the Nichols lawyers' public pressure attempt, my response to the press was simple: "A no contest plea allows a defendant to be sentenced by a judge without actually taking responsibility for the acts of which he is accused. I think that speaks for itself." The trial was about taking responsibility and a no contest plea circumvented that.

Closure

At long last, the state murder trial for Terry Nichols started in March of 2004. It was held in the forested, rolling hills of southeastern Oklahoma, in the small city of McAlester, a town of under 20,000 people that had enjoyed a surprising number of famous residents ranging from country singer Reba McEntire to U.S. Speaker of the House Carl Albert.

The trial itself would take place in the sprawling courtroom of District Judge Stephen Taylor. Since McAlester was a couple of hours drive from Oklahoma City, logistics dictated we open up a small office across the street from the courthouse. It was quite an undertaking. Three attorneys—Sandra Stensaas Elliott, Lou Keel, and Suzanne Lister; three support staff—Robyn Mayes, Jill Butler, and Donna Reed; and one investigator from the Oklahoma City Police Department, Mark Easley, made the long haul. There were so many metal file cabinets filled with trial information that we had to have carpenters strengthen the rented space's floor beneath them, lest they potentially break through into the basement beneath the building.

After the trial's media event beginning, the courtroom was rarely packed to the gills as was usual for the earlier federal cases, unless a witness of particular interest was known to be coming. The people of McAlester were truly lovely to both my staff and to the many victims' families and survivors that came to watch the trial. The downtown Baptist church was particularly wonderful as each day they provided something of a sanctuary for these individuals, some of whom had traveled a far distance to see Terry Nichols on trial for the death of a loved one.

It was a significant hardship on our staff to move there for months, but there was no way we could simply commute. They were all volunteers, none having been ordered to participate in the case, and all being dedicated and emotionally attached to the many victim families and survivors they had come to know and love over the years of their involvement with the case. We added rent houses and furniture to the growing list of expenses coming out of my existing office budget. We tried as best as we could to minimize the loneliness and sacrifice of living away from their loved ones. One routinely "cynical-at-all-things-prosecutor" weekly Oklahoma City paper later chastised us for having had the audacity to get cable television for the rent houses, as if we were trying to rip off the good citizens of Oklahoma and had nothing better to do than sit around watching the Food Channel. They hadn't bothered to learn that my staff couldn't even get television reception without cable but, in retrospect, they would probably have begrudged them even that simple luxury.

The trial finally concluded in June after hundreds of witnesses and exhibits. The jury quickly concluded he was guilty of one hundred and sixty one counts of murder as well as counts of arson and conspiracy to commit arson (two of the three charges concerning the unborn children had been prevented from presentation to the jury for legal reasons). Now it was time for them to decide his punishment.

While we awaited the jury's decision, we watched Ronald Reagan's funeral procession on a small television set in our makeshift McAlester office. It was a huge event, befitting a man who had been one of my heroes. The federal government had been willing to shut down all of its offices for a day to honor the dead former president. Tens of thousands of people received a paid day off at a cost of millions. As I sat before the television I couldn't help but ponder the irony of it all. Two significant expenditures of money. One to honor a single, great life, another to honor one hundred and sixty three lives whose prospective greatness was cut short by madness. In the end, we pay for what we deem important.

Yet, when it came to reaching a decision as to punishment, the jury was unable to do so. In Oklahoma, only a jury can impose the death penalty so if they "hang up" and are unable to decide, the judge determines the sentence but only between "life" and "life without parole." Death is no longer an option. I had prayed for Nichols to be found guilty and that justice would be served; in the entirety of my career I had never asked God to intervene with a certain punishment—whether death or traffic fine. I understood full well God's thoughts on justice. I felt confident praying that. It was the sentencing piece that I typically avoided in prayer. On the subject of punishment I never felt comfortable giving God a closing argument.

Two months later, the judge sentenced Nichols to life in prison without parole.

Tuesday, August 10, 2004

Terry Nichols was formally sentenced yesterday. He gave a statement to the court in which in some way he expressed regret for what happened and then went on a lengthy course talking about Jesus, including a statement about God having delivered him from a death sentence. I was sitting next to Bob Macy out in the audience, who turned and whispered to me, "The phony S.O.B." I really don't know what to think about all that, God delivering him and all. Nichols claims to be a Christian but fortunately it's not my job to figure that out. The press asked me what I thought of some of what he said. I responded with a couple of thoughts about how the Bible refers to how we will be known by our fruit, thus we'll just have to wait and see what fruit Nichols produces. I also said something about how repentance goes hand-in-hand with confession and I'll look forward to see if he is willing to do that.

I am resolved to all of this—the verdict and everything. I placed it in the hands of the Lord. I'll not now whine having done so.

I was resolved but that didn't mean I didn't have moments of wanting to pull my hair out. Within a few days of the trial's end, one of the jurors dropped by our McAlester office as my staff was packing up to move back to Oklahoma City. He was deeply frustrated and upset by the jury's failure to impose the death sentence. He was especially frustrated with one female juror who he said had lied to us during the jury selection process by telling us she could, under the right circumstances, consider the death penalty. Once it came time to consider death, she had resolutely refused to do so, finally telling angry fellow jurors that she had been willing to say whatever she needed to say because she had wanted to be on *that* jury very badly. When she had been unwilling to even consider death as an option, three other wavering jurors ultimately decided to vote likewise, being strengthened by her obstinacy.

This was the sort of report to which I could only shake my head. In some respects it did not surprise me, nor would it likely surprise anyone hanging around any courthouse for very long. There are just some jurors who will say anything they think will either get them on or off a jury. That is just the way things are, whether in trials of grand national interest, or small trials of no interest at all. Right or wrong, jurors always tend to act predictably unpredictably human, and there is not a thing we can do about it. The battle was over.

I think, in the end, that much of life's battles are as much internal as external. I learned a great deal about responsibility in the Nichols case, and the battle to get him to accept responsibility or be held responsible was as much a battle within myself as it was in the public eye. We all have those battles, those opportunities to be tested and determine what we are willing to do in the face of opposition. What hill are we willing to die on? No matter what the size of your arena, there is a price to be paid for the privilege of leadership.

There comes a point of numbed acceptance to the fact that with responsibility comes decision and with decision comes division and with division comes opposition. What is it that brings us through that? What helps us to be the leaders we know we should be, even if it is costly? In my minor realm as district attorney, I was only experiencing what others have always experienced whatever the size of their realm. In that role I came to the stark realization that often the quality of our leadership decisions is less about actually knowing precisely what to do in a given situation and more about identifying the hill of principle upon which we might possibly die. It is the hill upon which we must be *willing* to die if we are to live a life of no regrets, even knowing there will be those who celebrate our funeral. The leaders to pity are not those who don't know what to do in each and every circumstance, but those who are afraid to choose a place to make their stand and possibly die.

George Müller was one of my great heroes of faith. He once wrote, "I had a secret satisfaction in the greatness of the difficulties which were in the way. So far from being cast down on account of them, they delighted my soul." That belief only came to Müller from the rich experience of being a faithful friend to God. Even as I ponder Müller's words, I suddenly realize that I am coming bit by bit to a place of no longer seeing obstacles in my path, but opportunities. That is a gift from God, a gift long in the making. A gift he has for all of us.

On the final night in McAlester, as we gathered in the Baptist Church in the aftermath of that long struggle toward justice, I stood alone for a moment just watching the milling figures of my staff and the many victims' family members that had assembled there. I'll never forget the adult daughter of a woman killed in the blast. She walked up to one of my prosecutors, hugged her and said "Thank you. Up until now, nobody had been convicted for the murder of my mother."

It was a good hill upon which to die.

"Blessed is the man who perseveres under trial; because when he has stood the test, he will receive the crown of life that God has promised to those who love Him" (James 1:12).

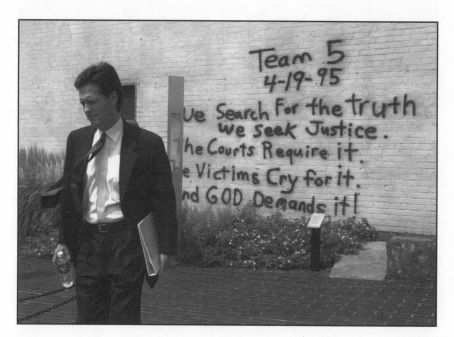

District Attorney Wes Lane on September 5, 2001 walking to address the local and national press concerning his decision to continue the prosecution of the Terry Nichols case. Wall writing was by rescue team members in the aftermath of the Murrah building bombing April 19, 1995. AP photo by J. Pat Carter.

Wes and Lori Lane with Derrick Haught in their first Christmas photo as a family, December 1994. At the present time, Derrick is an Oklahoma County Deputy Sheriff and Chinook helicopter pilot for U.S. Army National Guard.

PART IV
THE WALK OF DESTINY

There are plans and then there are PLANS. It is not God's will that we live lives of frustrated insignificance—and then we die. He knows the PLANS he has for us and they are adventurous, meaningful and deeply fulfilling. But such paths require more than mere intellectual assent to an experience. They require commitment. Other than our salvation, the best things in life are never free.

CHAPTER TEN

COUNTERING CULTURE

The path of Christian maturity demands we seek to emulate Jesus. Yes, Jesus is love and all about love . . . Our challenge comes when we realize that out of his great love, Jesus had a habit of making enemies because he dared to take stands. Stands that in the end got him killed.

Blessed are you when they revile and persecute you, and say all kinds of evil against you falsely for My sake. Rejoice and be exceedingly glad, for great is your reward in heaven, for so they persecuted the prophets who were before you. You are the salt of the earth; but if the salt loses its flavor, how shall it be seasoned? It is then good for nothing but to be thrown out and trampled underfoot by men. You are the light of the world. A city that is set on a hill cannot be hidden. Nor do they light a lamp and put it under a basket, but on a lampstand, and it gives light to all who are in the house. Let your light so shine before men, that they may see your good works and glorify your Father in heaven.

—Matthew 5:11–16

Mean Old Lane Doesn't Love the Precious Children

It was early afternoon when I first learned of the baby shower scheduled to take place in a couple of hours in my conference room. The "big" conference room is located next to the personal office of the district attorney. It was common for functions to take place there, from lawyer meetings to birthday parties. But this was different because the scheduled event would become a news story on both radio and television. Not the baby shower itself, but the fact that I cancelled it.

Once again, I had been DA for far less than a year when yet another "opportunity" for public adversity took place. As stated earlier, I spent almost six years of my prosecutorial career in charge of our juvenile division. I requested the job at juvenile out of the profound impact a fatherless little boy of ten had on my life. I witnessed the difficulties experienced by his dear mother in raising this child born out of wedlock with no one to help. Initially, I had no intention of becoming a "father" to this boy, but I kept finding myself envisioning him a few years later getting involved with gangs and the like and finally being dragged in handcuffs to a fifth floor courtroom. I looked at the precious, innocent little kid and melted. I became "Dad." In many ways, my experience of meeting Derrick was life changing for both of us. I would never have volunteered to go to the juvenile division had I not met him, and that experience convicted me that the breakdown of the family structure and the failure to cultivate value systems (character development) was, in great measure, at the root cause of crime. Civil societies throughout history have diminished or disappeared when these two things are missing.

In thousands of cases at the juvenile division I observed that the single greatest common denominator of these cases was the absence of a responsible father. The vast majority of the cases involved single parent families. The out of wedlock birth rate was spiraling (and continues to). Whole communities were in disintegration as young boys, without responsible, loving fathers, ran amuck in neighborhoods hunting other male associations we call gangs. I distinctly recalled one African American pastor friend of mine being very angry about this breakdown of family and responsibility. He said, "When I was a boy every one of my neighbors had the right to spank my behind if I caused trouble!" The issue to him was not about spanking; it was about the increasingly chaotic family structures and community reluctance to cultivate and enforce core values, both of which were increasing the risk of a child's inability to achieve his or her life potential.

The statistics surrounding the outcomes of out of wedlock births was alarming. The birth mothers were often very young, unable to complete an education, and consigned to a life of poverty. Their children were at increased risk of engaging in delinquent acts. The facts spoke for themselves. It was nothing personal; it was what it was. But, in many respects, it was grossly politically incorrect to speak negatively of single parent families. After all, "People" magazine touted movie stars like Jodi Foster and others and their out of wedlock births on its cover. The underlying message was always celebratory: "Aren't these people cool, and isn't independent birth mother life wonderful?" I always wondered how many young girls walked through grocery store checkout lines, saw that cover story and received the message that if it is okay for Hollywood, it must be okay for them too. Of course, these children weren't starlets and didn't have fat checkbooks.

So on that afternoon when I happened to discover that the Oklahoma County District Attorney's conference room—*my* conference room— was being used to celebrate an out of wedlock birth, I cancelled it immediately. It was as though my juvenile delinquency experience was screaming at me, "If you let this happen, you are condoning conduct that has statistically proven to be very damaging to thousands of children!" I had been giving a speech for several years entitled "Mixed Messages" regarding the damaging messages our culture sends our children, and one example was out of wedlock births! I found myself almost panicky that I might appear to be sending one of those mixed messages myself. My sole regret from the experience was the shock wave it sent through my staff as many doubtless concluded I was heartless. I even tried to explain my reasoning to the baby's father, but how could I do that without treading on his private life? All the poor guy could do was just sit there. I was his boss, and how intimidating was that anyway? What was he supposed to say? *Oops, we were just celebrating what they do on the cover of People.* It was an impossible situation and even with twenty-twenty hindsight I don't know how I could have cushioned the matter with my staff on two hours notice. Or for that matter, two days notice.

Then the public hailstorm began. It was my first experience of being publicly lambasted. In the Terry Nichols matter I was just being criticized, but this, on the other hand, was ridicule. It all came home that very same evening as I sat in my office numbly listening to myself being the topic of conversation on the top news talk station. I was the "question of the day," as they called it, and the question of the day was "Did Wes Lane do the right thing in cancelling a baby shower in his office?" It was the evening drive segment and the calls were coming in fast and furious. The station was actually taking a poll! I vividly remember sitting frozen to my chair, staring like a zombie at dust particles as they floated lazily on the shafts of light coming through the window blinds. It is a bizarre experience to be both in the listening audience *and* hear one's self being chastised by the callers. "Who does that guy think he is? Doesn't he like children?" Or, "that's the dumbest thing I've ever heard of!" On and on and on.

But I was defiant in my conviction. Speaking for years about our culture of "tolerance" had deeply convicted me to the "big picture" danger. We were tolerating everything anyone wanted to do even if it was killing us. Moral relativism reigned. As a society we were standing for *everything* and consequently *nothing* at all. I was determined not to send a mixed message. I called in to the station and talked on the air with the host, Mike McCarville (who as a good host was being neutral), and spouted off the statistics concerning out of wedlock births and how as district attorney I was *not* going to ratify conduct that I fully well knew harmed our society and even contributed to crime. This was not about whether Wes Lane loves children (which was the syrupy, simplistic and dishonest direction some wished to take it), but it was about taking a stand on a broader, politically incorrect, issue. I was amazed to later discover the callers were seventy-five percent on my side of the question.

The next day the television stations started showing up. The scene was actually taking on a carnival atmosphere as a soon-to-be political opponent arrived at the receptionist desk with a baby gift and TV cameras, denouncing my calloused regard for babies for the evening news. Eventually, the matter lost public interest and died away.

The experience dramatically proved to me the difficulty of taking a well-meaning stand on a critical issue on the one hand, and "getting along" with everybody on the other.

As I shared at the outset of this book, I, like most folks, have always wanted to be liked. I am still working on getting over that (at least the part that is inconsistent with pleasing God). I am much better at it than I used to be. We humans are social creatures and it usually pains us when we are rebuffed in some way. As I grew past adolescence into my teens and twenties, I realized that I got along quite well with people generally. Even when I was a young, beginning assistant district attorney engaging in combative jury trials, I still got along well with my opponents (the lawyers, not the criminally accused). Upon my return to that office in 1987, everybody within my sphere of influence at some point came to realize that I was a "practicing" Christian. I never tried to cram that down anyone's throat, nor did I hesitate to share Christ if the situation was appropriate. I never had a problem with anyone. I was Wes Lane, Nice Guy.

However, the strangest thing happened when I became *the* district attorney. Everything seemed to change.

Voodoo Dolls and Big Parties

Actually, to be more precise, things did not really *change* so much as the realities of life came into sharper focus, such as the intersection of my desire to be liked with the reality of people usually only being willing to accept people who pose no threat to their worldview. My territory, as it were, had increased as had the size of my bully pulpit. What I was saying around the office used to not make the front page. Now it did. The moment I told the press (at the governor's press conference announcing my appointment) that "I am particularly grateful to my God" for the job and continued to speak of an ongoing relationship with Christ during subsequent interviews, well, some folks got uncomfortable. It wasn't hard to figure out (especially when they publish disparaging cartoons) that in the view of some, I was automatically just one more religious nut trying to impose my morality on someone else. But wait! What was the big deal? Wasn't I the same Wes Lane I was when I was *not* the boss? Why am I suddenly catching grief? In fact, had I not mentioned the word "God" and kept the relationship between us a secret, at least one weekly rag might have actually printed nice stories about me. Well, probably not.

As it turned out over the next few years, God would cure me of being overly concerned about whether everybody liked me.

Today, many Christians live in subtle fear. This is not the life threatening kind of fear Christians suffer in many foreign countries because of their faith. Rather, it is the fear of not being accepted or seen as one of the "in" group. We fear not being popular with certain crowds. We fear being seen as a "zealot" or "judgmental" (that's a big one) or "out of touch" with modern society. We see photographs of people attending big parties looking happy and something within us yearns just a wee bit to be accepted by the "Hollywood" of our own community. I know that because I looked at those pictures, too, and experienced the same yearnings. Certainly, unless the desire becomes an idol, there is absolutely *nothing* wrong with going to those parties or hanging out and being friends with neat and successful people.

Here is my personal test on whether I might have an idol-in-the-making. It is when I see or hear something that in my heart-of-hearts (my spirit) I know that God does *not* like, yet, despite having the opportunity to speak to the matter and influence the culture with my opinion, I remain deafeningly silent out of my fear that someone will think me weird. At that very point in time, I become a co-conspirator to the matter troubling my heart in the first place. I have become a part of the problem by my silence. I allow my fear to rule me and I exalt the opinion of others more than that of God. That is modern idolatry no less than if I hung voodoo dolls from the door of my hut and sang praise songs to them. We worship what we value most.

I never realized how important it was for me to speak out until I actually did. What's more (and I know this may shock some Christians out there), there exists an entire segment of our population that doesn't necessarily claim Christianity but possesses strong moral values. And they are every bit as fearful as are we of speaking out.

I first noticed the importance of speaking out in the mid to late 1990s when addressing a large secular audience at a "Mayor and Government Leaders" conference on character in Indiana. The conference was about the intentional cultivation of character in our workplaces, our schools and our society. I was an assistant district attorney at the time and I was talking about our society's cultivation of young murderers like those killing their classmates at schools in Colorado and Arkansas. I discussed a number of examples of how we as parents had been presiding over the demise of our children's potential through the mixed messages we were sending out of our fearful political correctness. One quote I particularly liked that pointed out the growing inanity of our society was from syndicated columnist Mona Charen in the aftermath of one of the school shootings. In case you've not heard of Marilyn Manson, he is a particularly twisted performer glorifying death (Marilyn Monroe represents death by suicide, and Charles Manson represents death by homicide; thus, "Marilyn Manson"). Here is what Charen wrote: "Why is it that a nation recently willing to spend billions of dollars to keep children from inhaling cigarette smoke can shrug its collective shoulders when kids ingest the likes of Marilyn Manson? Until we confront our moral agnosticism, until parents demand an end to cultural pollution, we will not see an end to the carnage."

After about thirty minutes of encouraging this secular audience of leaders to find their voice and stop being afraid to go against the grain of Hollywood values, I found myself facing a standing ovation! I was quite surprised I hit such a nerve. In talking with a number of conferees afterwards, it became apparent that my mere willingness to speak out on what I believed to be "the obvious" had a liberating effect upon them, for they realized they were not the only ones thinking that way after all. There was some crazy guy from Oklahoma telling them they were right all along and that they were being a part of the problem if they didn't do something about it. It was a personal revelation to me to learn there were many people who shared my opinion. They were just waiting on someone to speak out because they were fearful about being the first one. I guess everybody wants to see if the first guy gets stoned.

I saw this sense of relief time and time again as I brought that message to many different groups. After becoming district attorney a few years later, what was especially interesting was becoming acquainted with and learning that even prominent and successful community leaders (who were so often featured in those big party photographs) felt the same fear and were waiting like everyone for someone else to strike the first blow. People are the same everywhere and are living in fear.

Worth Spit

As Christians we are supposed to be in the business of trying to be Christ-like.[1] We even assert to our fellow believers that we "want to be like Jesus." Occasionally we wear cute wrist bands that say "W.W.J.D.," standing for "What Would Jesus Do?" The bad news is that Jesus lost friends and followers like rats off a sinking ship over the positions he took. We delude ourselves if we think we are going to get a better deal.

When we take stands there *will* be opposition. We fool ourselves if we think we are loved because of our neutrality. Actually, we are not loved at all but rather tolerated, for that "love" swiftly degenerates once we speak the truth. Satan only loves us for playing the fool. Let's be honest, the upside of "playing the fool" is that the Enemy might not pick on us if we are living such an eternally insignificant existence anyway. We simply do not matter in the big picture, and he may not wish to waste his time by waking us up.

But wait, some say, *we must not be judgmental! Who are we to say what is right and what is wrong?* But we are not saying that. People confuse that it is "us" saying anything at all. Remember, this is not Susie's opinion or Bob's opinion on gay marriage, pornography, racism or widows and orphans and the poor. No, *it is God's opinion.* All we need to do is decide what value we are willing to place on the Bible as being the "Word" of God, in other words, on the Bible being God's "opinion" on a wide range of subjects. If we place a low value on it, then there is no point in taking stands on issues in conflict with God's opinion as expressed in the Bible. What would be the point? If on the other hand we place a high value on the Bible as God's opinion, then we need to decide whether our actions are consistent with the value we claim to have placed on Scripture.

I am often reminded of that event I spoke of earlier in the book, that moment of truth when I was confronted by Wayne Marley's sobering question, "So Wes, what is it you do? Just tear those pages from the Bible that are inconvenient with your lifestyle?"

The honest answer being yes, I had deluded myself believing I placed a high value on Scripture because my actions completely betrayed me. My conduct actually reflected utter hypocrisy, and we know what Jesus thought of Pharisees and white washed tombs and other hypocrites.[2] Even in later years of Christian life, as I hold deep beliefs about God's opinion on certain matters, there have been times I have failed to speak out on important things and acquiesced to my silence. I still live two lives. I'm working not to.

As Christians, we just need to be honest. If we call ourselves "followers of Jesus," then let's follow! If we are not really following, maybe we should stop calling ourselves "followers" or "Christians." I think Jesus would respect us more if we just came out and said "I don't believe this or that" as opposed to saying one thing and doing another (or standing silent). Jesus warned us there would be division,[3] so what do we think we are protecting ourselves from?

But wait! I thought Jesus was love and all things warm and fuzzy? Jesus may be all about love, but he sure had a knack for upsetting people. He was hardly successful as a people pleaser! We forget that Jesus came to destroy the works of the Devil[4] and (try not to wince when I say this) he considers those who won't take a stand as being worth only spit: He said, "I know your works, that you are neither hot nor cold. I could wish you were cold or hot. So then, because you are lukewarm, and neither cold nor hot, I will vomit you out of my mouth" (Rev. 3:15–16).

But what helps us to be taken seriously as Christians and not simply culture complainers is to take Christ seriously when he pointed out the two greatest commandments in Matthew 22:36–39. Love usually being easier said than done, the top two commandments, according to our Lord, are first, to love God, and second, to love people. Many of us focus on loving God but don't consider that doing so demands we pursue that second, especially uncomfortable commandment about loving people. Jesus did not hesitate to get his hands dirty touching people's lives in their area of felt need. Dealing with such needs gets messy and sometimes we as Christians are reluctant to do that. That alone can be intimidating, much less speaking out on our faith as I've been discussing. But we can't pick and choose. If we are not clearly touching both areas, if we are not engaging the culture on every front, we lose credibility when we take on the dangerous culture of tolerance. We are long on talk and short on example. Jesus didn't just give speeches about his disgust with the Pharisee culture; he dared to heal the hearts wounded by that culture as well.

At first, I was deeply hesitant to become the father to a fatherless boy and raise him to manhood. But now having done so, it was a life-changing privilege and now strengthens my ability to speak out with conviction and authority concerning the broken families of this toxically tolerant culture. I suspect Jesus knows full well that loving people as you love yourself is consistently challenging. Perhaps another time I'll tell you about the first time I set foot (as the sitting District Attorney of Oklahoma County no less) in a prison yard to minister the love of God to the inmates. They were shocked to see me and I was more than a little concerned how they might express themselves once they got over their shock. But it was a marvelous experience and underscored both by my belief in the importance of holding people accountable for their crimes, as well as walking the walk concerning my belief that the greatest societal crime prevention program kicks in when the criminal heart is changed for Christ. We must love God, love people, and push back darkness. All of which are action opportunities inviting an omnipotent Father to pour his supernatural self into his radiant purpose for our lives.

As in everything else in this walk with God, it is all about heart. Jesus understands our anxieties. He experienced anxieties himself. He even asked God if there might be a "plan B" to the cross.[5] But Christ's heart overrode his human reluctance as he first sought God's will on the matter. God's desire is for us to be salt and light (Matt. 5:11–16); he wants us to change the flavor of our atmosphere, to change the taste of our surroundings. That requires our stepping up and being counted. If you are intimidated at the thought, tell God your fears on the subject and say you are willing to have your heart strengthened. He is all about that.

Furthermore, I don't necessarily mean that the only way to serve God is to grab a megaphone at the next pro-life rally (unless that is where the Holy Spirit is directing you). It may be as simple as speaking up when seeing your friend glowing over a story in "People" magazine about another "love child" being spun off by some glamorous and temporary Hollywood relationship. Maybe you can share a few factoids about the damage this is doing to our culture. Be sensitive to your audience; sometimes a factoid will be much more effective than a Bible verse. Remember, I didn't call up the radio station on the subject of the baby shower in order to quote a verse. I called up to quote societal statistics. My faith informed my values, but my values were backed up by more than just biblical truths. These statistics actually backed up a principle at the heart of which stood my Christian belief system. Jesus said we need to exercise some wisdom as we engage culture. "Behold, I send you out as sheep in the midst of wolves. Therefore, be wise as serpents and harmless as doves" (Matt. 10:16).

I know we each have different giftings. I would never expect my shy wife, Lori, to grab a megaphone and speak to a crowd (that would truly take a miracle), but I would never be surprised to see her show up at a gathering to express her opinion by her presence. There are many ways to influence the culture surrounding us. In the end, what counts is whether or not we took a stand. We are all standing somewhere, and the question is, are we standing *with Jesus*?

As I have said, we all wish to be liked, and we came by that desire honestly. We just need to beware that our natural desire to be liked does not morph into appeasement. Appeasement has always been a poor deterrent to a determined enemy, for we are still destroyed in the end. There are no negotiations with the Devil; no neutrality when it comes to his value system of "steal, kill and destroy."[6] Value systems that result in the destruction of institutions created by God (such as marriage and family) demand a response. When we stand silent in the face of the destruction of such a value system, we are not staying out of an argument. We are taking sides with the aggressor. We collaborate with the Enemy. It is tough to be both invisible through silence and to operate at the same time as salt and light to our community.

An "Open Hand"

Sometimes we also have a tendency to forfeit ground we don't have to forfeit. As we live in a culture of fear, we often fail to take advantage of the law, even when it is on our side. A good case in point is when we lead an office in business or government, and yet we're afraid to breathe that we are Christians or allow those who are to thrive in that office. We mistakenly believe that Christians—or other faiths—are not allowed to meet or express themselves in our workplace.

There are many professing Christians working in the Oklahoma County District Attorney's Office. When I was the district attorney I gave them the freedom to gather and have meetings, just as I would have allowed any other faith group. The law says that if we open the office up to one group, we must open it up to all. In my office we would regularly have luncheons at which well known individuals could come and give their Christian testimony. Football greats like Josh Heupel and Paul Blair came to speak, as well as business greats like the founders of Hobby Lobby, David and Barbara Green. Television and Christian music personalities, and many others came to encourage members of my staff as they walked out their faith. Nobody was compelled to attend; it was simply an open invitation. Many came and many did not. Attendance was their choice and no one ever took roll. I did not organize these meetings or even personally invite staff to them. I just allowed people to exercise their constitutional right to meet. We simply chose to be neither afraid nor embarrassed about who we were.

Life is all about choices. The destiny we have in God is all about choices. I feel pretty confident in saying that God is watching to see what choices we will make. It is not our job to worry or fret about what friends or status we may or may not lose when we make those choices. God is the one who controls those issues. Our responsibility is to be faithful. We need to hold our friends, our jobs, our very lives with an "open hand."

Kent Humphreys is the president of an organization called "Christ at Work." This is an international Christian businessmen's association. I once heard him make a remarkable statement in the aftermath of having lost a multi-million dollar account in his own business. The interviewer asked him how he handled this kind of loss, and Humphreys's response was profound. Essentially, he said he knew that as a follower of Christ all blessings came from the Lord and that he made a point of holding his clients with an "open hand." In other words, he would do everything he possibly could to responsibly deal with and keep clients, but ultimately he realized that when it all came down to the bottom line, not everybody was called to be his clients or to remain his clients. In his loss of that multi-million dollar account, he chose to trust God and would not lose heart over losing a grip on that which was not his in the first place.

This same "open hand" principle applies to our friends, our jobs, and our positions. We are his servants. God knows our needs and is fully Lord over our circumstances. I paid a price politically over my allowing those Christian meetings to take place in my office. I was the subject of some very nasty stories being passed around about how I *made* people attend those meetings and that if an employee was not a Christian then they could not get promoted within the office. It was utter nonsense. But I didn't go whining about it because I knew there would be a price to be paid. I had counted the cost. Yet I also knew that when we dare to put God in charge of our business, our career, our family—our very lives—that God is fully capable of taking care of us. I did not look upon my political position as something I needed to grasp with a clenched fist; rather it was something to hold with an open hand. God was in charge. We fight the good fight, we fight to win, but God will handle the rest. He is in charge of the results. What a relief that I do not have to worry about who or what I lose in God's economy.

Stove Toads

I have already discussed the fear with which many of us are afflicted. Look at the bright side—we may be fearful, but at least we are feeling *something*. At least our consciences are being tweaked at some level, and there is a tacit recognition of a problem. Dead people, however, are oblivious to fear.

What I refer to as *stove toads* (also known as the "living dead") are those of us so caught up in our own thing that we are either blissfully ignorant of the cultural disintegration around us or we just plain don't much care. Maybe we mildly complain about this or that, but we are mostly just mouth when we do so. After all, it's not as though a bomb went off in *our* neighborhood. Our defeat has been far more subtle than that. By way of explanation, let me teach you how to cook a live toad. First or all, you cannot cook a live toad by tossing him into a pot of boiling water because he'll just jump out. What you can do, however, is put the toad in a pot of water at room temperature, turn the stove on low, and that toad will sit there in that comfortable pot and cook to death contentedly. *Ahhhhh, what a nice warm bath this is. I think I'll just sit here awhile . . . my, my . . . I'm not feeling my toes but I really don't care . . . hmmm, now I don't feel my body but isn't this pleasant? Hmmm, things are getting a bit dark in here.*

We have slowly but surely grown numb to our own impending, incremental doom. In the end, we won't even know what hit us. Hence, we have become a nation of stove toads. Consider this as a proof. Many of us are largely indifferent to what is on television. We don't say much or complain. Perhaps we restrict our children, perhaps we do not (and statistically we know that the average child is watching a stunning amount of television). Yet what if we were able to record a few days worth of television (including young people's favorites like MTV and VH1) and then send that recording back to about 1960 so our grandparents could take a look? What do you think their response would be? Contented "stove toad" silence? They would be reaching for their shotguns and marching in the streets. Politicians would be hounded and advertisers boycotted. I suspect a number of parents would be taken to task as well. Our grandparents would be appalled that children are actually watching the crude things constantly broadcast on television, much less the fact that it is even allowed on the air. Not having been slowly "cooked" like the toad, they would be jumping mad.

If we agree that a good percentage of that which on television is morally offensive, let's remember this happened on our watch, didn't it? Frank McPherson, the former CEO of Kerr-McGee Corporation, made this chilling remark: "We are responsible for the cultural decline that takes place on our watch." He is right, and obviously we did not do enough to stop it. I could go on at length about the moral belief systems our children are developing by watching too much television, but that is not within the scope of this work. What is really sad is that there will be a good number of people taking offense to my remarks because they see nothing at all wrong with where our culture is going. They see our society only as becoming increasingly "enlightened." We are "People magazine people," good, often hard working, well-meaning citizens just like everybody else. And we are also stove toads who are so dead to the problem we don't even realize it.

Do you remember the Jabez prayer?[7] We each have a territory, and we pray that Jabez prayer asking God to bless us and expand our territory. But how much decline did the territory we are *currently* stewarding experience while under our watch? Yet we petition God for *more* territory to steward into decline? Perhaps your "territory" is your family, your neighborhood or workplace, or anything else. In the final analysis, if we died tomorrow, what difference will we have made besides just being a nice person? Did we flavor the atmosphere with our saltiness? Were we beacons of light? Did our friends or co-workers ever see us take a stand costing us anything? Did anyone, including our own children, ever stop fearing being "politically incorrect" because they had us as role models for truth?

Perhaps another way of looking at it is that if we were charged with the crime of "being a salty Christian," would there be enough evidence for a jury to find us guilty?

Our goal must not be that we somehow come through life unscathed. I am not saying that the goal is to foment trouble in every direction. What I am saying is that as Christians we need to stop wearing camouflage. We need to stop being embarrassed about the team we signed up for.

I am an Oklahoma Sooner fan. I don't start getting mumbly-mouthed just because I run into a Texan. I am unabashed and will defend my team. I suspect the Lord would love it if some Christians would be as publicly ardent for the Kingdom as we are for our ball clubs.

The sign-up sheet, from Jesus' own mouth, reflects that we, as alleged disciples, need to consider the cost of membership. Signing up means being willing to take a stand even against our own mother and father and family if need be.[8] Make no mistake about it; there is a cost to discipleship. But as someone who has in a very miniscule way made a payment (as compared to the very great and dangerous cost paid by Christians in Muslim countries under threat of death for *their* stand), the return on the investment is remarkable in joy, peace, and the amazing love of an engaged God.

There is an old tale of the emperor who had no clothes. He was duped into believing he was wearing the most beautiful royal clothes ever made, and in his arrogance he ran around buck naked. Everyone knew the king was a fool, but nobody wanted to appear uncool by saying so. They placed a greater value on their position and personal popularity than on the truth. They wanted to be accepted *and* they feared the power structure. It took a small child to burst the bubble with his innocent declaration of the obvious truth, "He's naked!" to break the spell of fear and pride. Only then did the fearful many gain the courage to go out of step with the prevailing culture of foolishness.

In our culture today there are many emperors needing their spells broken, people hoping someone will finally speak the obvious truth and free them from their captivity of fear. All it takes is one person with childlike faith to break that spell by his or her willingness to step out in faith and speak the truth. Are you that person?

CHAPTER ELEVEN

DEFEAT AND DESTINY

Alice: *If I had a world of my own . . . Nothing would be what it is, because everything would be what it isn't. And contrary wise, what is, it wouldn't be. And what it wouldn't be, it would. You see?*[1]

What the world often sees as defeat, in God's eyes may actually be victory. Likewise, what the world may see as victory may often be viewed from a heavenly perspective as defeat. So long as we walk God's path, the world may well view us as failures and fools. But the reality of God is that we are both his faithful children and favored friends. God determines the times and seasons of where to place us and always has a reason for doing so. He does not waste his assets. He is relentlessly purposeful. His will for our lives is that we exist as conquerors and experience the victorious life.

The Opportunity of Defeat

Election night, November 7, 2006. I had just lost my bid for re-election by 821 votes in a total of 173,409 votes cast. The television cameras were seemingly insatiable. It had been a long and difficult campaign. Suffice it to say, politics is not for the faint of heart. I'll never forget walking the hallway of the hotel at which several campaigns were gathered and listening as my campaign manager, Holly Miller, received the returns over a cell phone. It had been back and forth, up and down all evening. In 2002, it seemed like our race was over almost as soon as the polls were closed, but not that night. The evening dragged on and on and on. Finally, Holly turned to me and breathed, "We lost."

It's hard to say what I was feeling just then. I was already exhausted and numb from the whole process. I just remember the clamoring press and my stoic Lori, standing a few feet away as I mouthed the words to her "I lost." It had been a bad night for Republicans across the country which, of course, was little consolation.

I learned during my five and one-half years as District Attorney for Oklahoma County that with virtually every major and even minor decision, somebody gets mad and another gets glad—and some seek to get even. A former district attorney made an interesting comment to the press in the aftermath of the election to the effect that often DAs have a shorter "shelf life" than other elected politicians for just that reason. I certainly knew I had acquired my fair share of hard core enemies.

But I had no regrets. The enemies I made were, as far as I was concerned, honorably earned.

That fall evening in 2006, as Lori and I faced the reality of my newly lost career, the reporters peppered me with the question, "So what you will do now?" (As though I had actually planned on losing and had a plan B). My response was one of a fellow who, though surprised and deeply disappointed, had seen way too much of a loving, faithful, and yes, *supernatural* God to panic. The only thing that came to mind before the cameras was two truths. First, my genuine gratitude for having had the privilege of serving as DA, and second, that God had *always* been faithful to me, far more than I had been to him. It was not my place to whine. How could I? Indeed, it had been an honor to serve at the pinnacle of my chosen field. Yet had that question been posed a decade earlier in my understanding of God, I'm not sure how I would have responded. Years earlier, I would have likely been consumed with thoughts like, "But I thought God wanted his servants in office! How could he have let me down like this?" Or, "Is he punishing me for something?" After all, is not the God of the Bible fully capable of influencing just a few hundred more votes? But on that November evening, I had seen way too much of God not to know his character very, very well. I had an idea of what was going on.

As Lori and I walked back to the room where my staff and supporters were waiting, we passed by a small room with large windows along the hallway. Earlier, there had been a constant group of people sitting, standing, and kneeling, all praying for me. A very humbling sight indeed. As I rounded the corner and entered the larger room filled with dejected and tearful friends, I knew that I had to say something. I had to tell them the truth. I didn't know if they would buy into it, but I know I certainly had. I told them the story of an old man looking back on his life. A life of much adversity and much blessing. A life filled with enemies and opposition and heartache. A man who had lived the supernatural life. It was the story of King David and his thirty-seventh psalm. It was a psalm looking back from the vantage point of an old man upon his long walk with a faithful God. David wrote, "The steps of a good man are ordered by the Lord, and He delights in his way. Though he fall, he shall not be utterly cast down; for the Lord upholds him with his hand. I have been young and now am old; yet I have not seen the righteous forsaken, nor his descendants begging bread" (Ps. 37:23–24).

Throughout that psalm David repeatedly urges us, "do not fret . . . do not fret . . . do not fret, it only causes harm." Quite a perspective for an old warrior scarred from many battles both physical and of the heart, and it was his perspective on life that I shared with the gathered crowd. On that night, knowing that somewhere across the city were those celebrating my political death, I did not have perhaps that grand level of faith found in the elderly David, but I certainly had experienced enough to know that David was speaking the truth and God had not abandoned me. He does not waste his assets. He is crazy about his kids, and I knew I was one of them. For that matter, a distant part of me recognized that he had actually been rather kind in my removal. It could have been a landslide.

But perhaps the very strongest sense I had that night stemmed from one more little thing I knew about my heavenly Dad, and that is he just loves to give tests. I knew good and well that evening the Lord was watching to see how I reacted to everything. I *knew* it was not only the viewing public watching me that evening. It was God. Here I had told him about a million times, "Lord, you send me wherever you want," and darn if he didn't take me up on the offer! Now, having been served a delicious dish of humble pie, I completely believed this was my last and final test in the office the Father had so graciously given me. I looked on this as my *opportunity*, not my defeat. Everything I had seen about God, everything I had learned about God, everything I had experienced about God had been crushed and distilled into one pointed, final, and crucial moment. It was the final exam question. My future was tied not to my office but to my relationship with God. I knew God had not been ambushed that evening, nor was he surprised. The Sovereign knew exactly what he was doing. My attitude in the face of what "the world" would view as disaster would reveal what I really *believed*. From my point of view, how I finished this exam would have an impact on whatever God's next assignment might be. What size "territory" did he think I could handle? The final exam question was quite simple really: *Will you trust me Wes, even if I publicly take away your career?*

As I look back on the battleground of my tenure as district attorney, I am so glad to have experienced the adversity. Yes, I really am sober as I write this. I think I can also see why the Bible says, "Your word is a lamp unto our feet and a light to our path."[2] I think if God had illuminated the entire five and a half year highway that Lori and I stepped into, we might have said, "Forget that, Lord, are you nuts?" Some things are best left in the dark lest we run away screaming.

The totality of the experience, from the divisive Terry Nichols case to nasty rumors[3] being spread around about Lori and substance abuse, to office decisions of literal life and death, to enemies willing to fabricate malicious lies to move their political ball downfield—it was like nothing we had ever experienced. There was no polite grace period. No honeymoon. It was as if someone fired the starting gun for the forces of adversity to be unleashed the moment I took the oath of office. The older I got, the more impressed I became, not with how smart I was, but with how utterly dependent I was upon God's wisdom and favor. I would frequently find myself telling the Lord that *surely* he did not want us *both* to look foolish—me for a poor decision and him for putting me in office. He never let me down. It was the greatest school I ever attended.

But if all of these experiences of adversity had served to challenge and build my level of faith, there was one event, however, that actually *shook* my faith to the core.

The Empire Strikes Back

Journal: Friday, October 12, 2001

Yesterday the Court of Criminal Appeals reversed the Dittmeyer case on a 3–2 vote. It took my breath away. I received the information as I was driving back from just having completed a speech at the OKC Golf & Country Club. I have been in a spiritual struggle trying to ascertain how to read this. Deep down, I think I know. When I got back to the office, and after the initial hullabaloo was over, I was still clearly struggling with the situation and how to process this in light of how the Lord had worked in my life and in that case particularly. Sheila stepped into my office, wagged her finger at me and simply said, "This is the Devil and you need to re-read that prophecy!" In other words, just because the Enemy has retaken a village, don't surrender the war. My spirits immediately lifted. The Lord has been very gracious to plant her alongside me.

My spirits might have lifted, but only momentarily. It was a stinging and bitter defeat. The Crystal Dittmeyer experience had been one of the most significant experiences in my walk of faith. Not only had the case been reversed by the slimmest of margins (a 3 to 2 vote), the major portion of evidence upon which we had been relying had been jettisoned by the court and forbidden for use in a subsequent trial. The complex series of circumstantially connected dots that convicted Ben Crider and shocked a courthouse had now lost a significant series of those dots. This case would prove to be my personal thorn in the flesh for the remainder of my tenure as I watched it further deteriorate into complete collapse as the last threads of evidentiary hope snapped and fell apart.

Our key witness, a person upon whose testimony it would be critical that the jury completely believe, had misled us on an issue. It was one of those issues that the court in the first trial had ruled inappropriate and irrelevant for the jury's ears. We had argued successfully that this matter the defense wished to inject into the trial was in the category of a red herring; it was something meant to distract the jury from focusing purely on whether the evidence presented established the defendant as the one who committed murder. It revolved around whether this witness had had an affair. If so, the defense wished to paint this un-identified lover as the possible killer of Crystal. Our witness adamantly denied the affair and our position was that not only did we believe our witness but that even had an affair taken place, there wasn't a single shred of evidence linking such an unknown individual with the death of Crystal.

DNA testing had radically improved since the late 1990s when we first tried the case, and in what we prosecutors thought would utterly eliminate the matter from further consideration, we sent a piece of evidence off for new testing. Much to our shock, the test established that not only had there been an affair but that our witness had lied to us. Not only us, but had lied under oath in 1996 when I had specifi-cally questioned her on the matter.

Unlike the infamous incident of the North Carolina DA, Mike Nifong, withholding DNA evidence from the defense in the Duke Lacrosse team rape allegations, we immediately provided that infor-mation to the defense, knowing it spelled doom for our case. The matter was further complicated, if that were possible, by the witnesses continued adamant denial of the affair. I knew that this new evidence was now going to be admitted into a subsequent trial for Crider and that with the witness continuing to deny the affair in the face of DNA evidence, her entire critical testimony was going to be disregarded by the jury as she would be utterly destroyed on the witness stand. It was impossible to explain away why she might lie about one area, but all the rest of her testimony was true. Crider was willing to plead guilty to a manslaughter charge and receive a ten year sentence, which roughly amounted to the time he had already been in prison. I was amazed that he was even willing to go that far.

Early in my tenure as district attorney I had established what I called a homicide committee in our office. It was a team of the most experienced homicide prosecutors in the office with between seventy-five and one hundred years of collective homicide prosecution experience. I made it a rule that before anyone could plead out a murder or manslaughter case they had to run the case down to the committee and explain why the case should not be tried by a jury. The courthouse reality was that occasionally younger, more inexperienced prosecutors got intimidated into pleading tough cases. I wanted that to stop. I wanted extreme consistency in the way we handled these cases, especially death penalty cases. Many a prospective plea deal had been rejected by this committee, and the prosecutor forced to trial (the committee was, therefore, not popular with the defense bar). Even though as DA I did not have to run one of my cases past this committee, I did not believe it was right to bypass it, and so my co-counsel and I reviewed the entirety of the case before them. The committee was unanimous in its belief that there was no way we could win. The extraordinarily difficult case with no body was simply too far gone. There were no further shreds of evidence. The opportunity to get Crider to accept some limited responsibility and become a convicted felon for life was all there was left. It was a pyrrhic victory at best.

In the Crystal Dittmeyer case, I learned not only what it was like to experience the gnawing heartache of defeat, but the later deeper heartache of having sincerely hurting individuals move from applause and gratitude to attack and recrimination. Most of Crystal's family understood the case reality, others did not. Then again there were those with darker motives seeking political gain from the memory of a dead child.

In the end, however, the buck stops with the man in charge—in this case me—and as a great and once greatly vilified president said, "If you can't stand the heat, get out of the kitchen."[4] It was not as though I had been forced to file the murder charge in a case with no body and no eyewitnesses; I volunteered for a war and war is ugly. We should never be surprised when we confront a determined opposition on a righteous quest. If it is not dangerous, there likely wasn't much to be fighting for in the first place. I would rather lose having fought the fight than look back upon a memory of having been too afraid to even try. The fight for Crystal was a just cause and another one of those hills worth dying on.

Yet the experience, for our purposes, also points out an important truth. Defeat always yields up an opportunity to choose our next path. We all have those forks in the road of faith; places where we find our faith shaken to the core and must decide what we will believe from that point on. A friend of Lori and mine, Cynthia, had an insightful thought on the subject of defeat and the sense of guilt that can accompany it. I was sharing my sadness over the Dittmeyer case final result when she looked at me and dryly commented, "Wes, when you won the case initially, you didn't take credit for the victory. You credited God. Now that the case went the other direction, why are you now claiming the defeat? I thought the case was God's?"

A profound thought.

If I should not have received credit for the victory, why was I so eager to claim credit for the defeat? I left no stone unturned, and there was absolutely *nothing* more I could have reasonably done as a prosecutor. I performed my role in the workplace to the best of my ability.

Yet, there is another role involved here besides the one in the workplace. It is the role in the Spirit. The lesson I learned during the Crider trial was that prayer matters and that it influences the workplace. There was an intensity of prayer from both myself and others that, as I shared earlier, influenced the outcome. Once the jury gave their verdict, however, the praying largely stopped, other than intermittent prayers of praise and gratitude. In retrospect, I can see that, whereas a battle had been won, there was still a war taking place. There was still an appeal to the Oklahoma Court of Criminal Appeals, a process that took about two years to complete. As they say, "It's not over until it's over." The principle I have drawn from this is that until our war finally is *over*, we cannot stop praying.

We need to distinguish between a short term battle and a much lengthier war. We are commanded to pray without ceasing.[5] Life is warfare, and we make a mistake when we think we can take a vacation. Our enemy is the Devil, and he is imminently patiently waiting for an opportunity.[6] Outcomes are not necessarily on autopilot. I do believe there is an evil out there whose name is Satan, and I do believe the Bible when it says his job is to steal, kill and destroy.[8] I also believe the will of God does not always come to pass when the humans upon whom he is relying to stand in the gap fail to do so.[9]

I am reminded of Edmond Burke's profound comment, "All that is necessary for the triumph of evil is for good men to do nothing." The spiritual equivalent would be, "All that it takes for evil to triumph is for good men and women to stand by and not pray."

Ultimately, and I want to be very clear on this, I do *not* know what role the failure to continue in aggressive prolonged intercession played. But I know that at trial I witnessed the miraculous and that after trial I witnessed defeat, and what was missing between points A and B was aggressive intercessory prayer. Maybe something else was at work there, something that really had nothing to do with me or prayer or whatever. I'm not God and I don't have the "big picture." Believe me, I'll look forward to asking the Lord someday. But there are principles of persistent prayer here that ought not be ignored as we exercise wisdom in the pursuit of God's destiny for our lives.

Regardless of the reasons, on that October 2001 morning, my faith in God was still severely shaken. I had a spiritual crisis taking place that was a huge threat to my walk with God. I was like a plane spinning to earth, its pilot trying desperately to get the plane to pull up without crashing. My entire "God experience" was under attack at its most vulnerable point. Defeat had taken place, and it is at times like this that we are presented with our moment of choice. It is our choice which fork in the road we will take—the path of belief and trust? Or the path of unbelief and doubt? Our choices influence our destiny. It is at those points that we must stop before deciding, pause and take a look behind us at the memorials left behind.

Memorials on the Road to Our Destiny

Memorials were so important to God that he instructed Joshua to set one up consisting of a heap of stones to mark where the Jordan River had been parted for the Israelites to cross over into the promised land.[10] God did not want them forgetting his faithfulness in bringing them to the place he promised he would. He knew they would have opportunities to forget, opportunities to lose heart, and opportunities to make poor choices at the fork in the road of belief. Memorials are encouragements from our past, reminding us that God has always been there for his people, often in remarkable ways. Memorials are restraints lest we choose the path of unbelief.

We are not the first of God's children to waiver in the face of opposition. Even the mighty David had his moments of hanging by faith's fingernails: He pled, "Do not deliver me to the will of my adversaries; for false witnesses have risen against me, and such as breathe out violence. I would have lost heart, unless I had believed that I would see the goodness of the Lord in the land of the living" (Ps. 27:12–13).

When my secretary confronted me upon my visible slide into the depths of despair over the Dittmeyer case that October morning, she strongly suggested I re-read a memorial I kept in my desk. It was something to remind me of God's faithfulness and awe-inspiring supernatural pathway. I recorded the words three different men spoke to me, words they believed God was sharing with them to reveal to me. All three were strangers to me, one even from another state. Two of them I met at a church function (not my church) and the third approached me at a luncheon. All of these meetings took place the preceding February, when I was an assistant district attorney directing the juvenile division, and when Bob Macy still had a couple of years left to his term of office.

The sum and substance of the three messages was that God was getting ready to change my assignment, that he had plans to promote me, and that I was being sent into the political arena where I would be forced into utter dependence on him.

I confess I had never been in a situation where anyone would presume to share God's mind about me on a matter. I found myself intrigued but unwilling to assume any of it was true. Still, I dutifully copied each man's words. If these messages were to be believed, *something was getting ready to change*. Furthermore, if my assignment *did* change, that would phenomenally underscore my belief that we as Christians are not celestial pin balls bouncing randomly about the universe, but rather lives that are ordered and directed by a living God. If the strangers' words were *not* from God, they were just so much noise and nothing would ever come of them.

Journal, Sunday, May 6, 2001

I am fasting today. A lot has happened in the last week. Last Monday, Bob Macy publicly announced his retirement effective June 30. The governor now appoints his successor. There has been a flurry of activity—getting people to write letters of support, etc. Lori and I had a long scheduled trip to Beaver's Bend down in Broken Bow. I needed that trip. I needed to get my focus on the Lord and not on the circumstances. There have been a number of negative reports that the governor wanted to appoint Mike Hunter (the current Secretary of State) to the job, because he wanted to appoint someone from outside the office due to the scandal at OCPD's lab.[11]

Standing out in a trout stream or sitting on a porch overlooking the river provided the opportunity to contemplate just where the Lord has taken me over the last few years, especially the last couple since the Dittmeyer case. I realized from my relationship with him that I will praise him no matter what the outcome. He taught me that a long time ago. I will keep my focus on the Lord and not on my circumstances. Sheila, who is my secretary at the juvenile division, told me last week that my staff couldn't believe how calm I was on Tuesday. I wasn't wringing my hands or being a basket case. She told me it was a real witness to them that I knew who was in command. The Lord has been carving a deep spiritual river in me and Lori. We have seen so much.

I am at a crossroads in my life. Something will change this summer . . .

The three men were proven right. Indeed, it was God sending that message through them; another supernatural experience underscoring there is much more of God out there than I previously believed.

I suspect one of the reasons God telegraphed the advanced clues from those three men was to make sure I would know to whom I needed to give the credit for my promotion (and as I've said, that is exactly what I did, although nobody knew the "three men reason" why I was so firmly determined to do so). It was both a profound taste of the supernatural life and an inoculation against pride. Members of the nominating committee later made clear to me that two weeks out from Governor Keating's announcement, there was "no way" (and I quote) I was going to get that job. So, here was a memorial in my life of where a real God had shown up, telling me in advance what was going to happen. I *knew* I had not done this on my own. I had not figured it out on the front end, but it was easy to connect the dots in the aftermath. The pieces to this became the paper in my desk that Sheila urged me to re-read after the Dittmeyer defeat. I needed to drink into my spirit the memorial reminding me that the Lord brought me to this party in the first place, and he would back me up if I would only trust.

Memorials keep us focused on God, reminding us that there is Someone out there actually in control. We do not live random lives. The Christian life is *supposed to be* different and set apart from the natural human life experience. It is supposed to be supernatural. Supernatural should be the *normal* Christian experience. At least it has been for me, Lori, and many people we know. We will *never* again settle for the sub-normal. No one should.

The Only Point of View that Really Matters

When I lost that election and had other opportunities to experience life's setbacks, on each occasion I have also had to decide how I was going to view myself in light of my circumstances, and from what source I would draw my esteem.

The way God sees us is so very different from the way we see ourselves. A tremendous example of this is the story of Gideon found in the book of Judges. The people of Israel were being greatly oppressed by a nomadic people called the Midianites. Every time the Israelites had two pennies to rub together, the Midianites would swoop in and steal them (the Israelites had actually put themselves in this position through their disobedience to God, but that is another story with another important truth). In chapter six of Judges, Gideon is hiding in a wine press trying to thresh out some wheat without the Midianites seeing him. Suddenly an angel (actually the Lord) appears to him and says: "The Lord is with you, you mighty man of valor!"

Gideon, apparently not listening, just starts whining and complaining about what was going on, how unfair it was, how God had forsaken them, blah, blah, blah. "Then the Lord turned to him and said, 'Go in this might of yours, and you shall save Israel from the hand of the Midianites. Have I not sent you?'" Gideon, apparently still not listening, continues to act the weenie, talking about what nobodies his family were, what a weak stick he was, blah, blah, blah.

To make a longer story shorter, Gideon finally becomes convinced about a very important matter; God's perspective on him was different from his own. How did Gideon view himself? As a nothing. How did God view him? As a "mighty man of valor." Why was he a mighty man of valor? Because in verse sixteen God gives him a clue: "And the Lord said to him, 'Surely *I will be with you* and you shall defeat the Midianites as one man'" (emphasis mine).

God would be *with* him in the pursuit of the destiny and calling God had on his life. This affair with the Midianites wasn't going to be about Gideon. *It was going to be about God.* When we commit ourselves to the destiny and calling God has on our lives, our success is no longer about us; rather, it is about God. We become the mighty man or woman of valor because *God is with us.* It is *his* strength, *his* power, and *his* plan. We have to realize that *it is God's reputation on the line*, not our own. We are sent by God, and we are heaven's ambassadors acting under the authority of a living Lord of Hosts. We need to stop regarding ourselves as filthy rags. That may be what we *were*, but it is not who we *are*. We have to remember who we are *in Christ*—sons and daughters of the King of kings, mighty men and women of valor.

Does this mean we will not suffer setbacks? No. Does this mean we won't experience suffering? No. The outcome is the Lord's and not our own. Getting rid of our concerns over our own personal reputations will go a long way towards absorbing that concept. Our effort should be toward aligning our point of view of ourselves with that of God's. Instead of self-esteem, it should be God-esteem.

I had to keep a grip on the correct point of view the night I lost my election and my prosecutorial career. I knew God loved and valued me. I knew he had always been faithful. Importantly, I knew I had been faithful as well. I *purposefully chose to remember* how it was that I became district attorney in the first place. It had been a supernatural experience from the beginning, and I *chose* to believe it so at the end. It is God's character to bless and not punish his faithful children. A perfect Father never beats an obedient child.

Two Last Thoughts

My constant enemy is fear. I suspect it is for most people (whether we like to admit that or not). I believe fear to be the single greatest obstacle to our achievement of the calling and destiny God has on our lives. It is a primary obstacle to our faith, and it is what holds us back. It is the ball and chain to our progress in God. Fear prevents us from stepping out in faith.

Fear of failure and of being accepted is at the heart of much of our personal struggles. This fear is often very subtle and difficult even to spot. I was once even surprised to realize that I had been putting off some of my devotional moments because I feared whether I would be able to replicate some of the profound moments I had experienced with God in the past! How subversive is that? Fear afflicts each of us, no matter what position we hold or what our sphere of influence might be. It is a constant fist fight from which we must not shy away.

As I have come to realize from experiences such as an election night defeat, or a major murder case reversal, discouragement is the Siamese twin to fear. They hang out together. They are a tag team meant to scuttle our hope in God. So here are two final thoughts on this road to the destiny God has for you and me. They each involve considerable messages brought through major men of God, Joshua and David.

Bucking Joshua

What a stud Joshua must have been! He was a real warrior. This man was nothing like Gideon, no mealy-mouth weenie talk out of Joshua. Yet, there is something very interesting about him with which God had to deal. In the first chapter of the book of Joshua, God makes very clear the destiny and calling he had for this warrior. He was to take the people of Israel into the Promised Land, the place they had waited decades to enter. Now remember, Joshua was a man who was Moses' personal assistant for many years. He saw God up close and personal, witnessing an unparalleled series of tremendous supernatural acts of God-wonder, things like seas parting, armies defeated, the whole nine yards. If anyone should have had unbelievably strong faith, it should have been Joshua. He had witnessed it all. God tells him in verse five, "No man shall be able to stand before you all the days of your life; as I was with Moses, so I shall be with you. I will not leave you or forsake you."

Have you ever noticed that in the same message God has to tell Joshua not once, not twice, but *three* times to be "strong and of good courage"? Three times? Was he just hard of hearing? God even has to add to that in verse nine: "Have I not commanded you? Be strong and of good courage; *do not be afraid, nor be dismayed*" (emphasis mine).

What's with that? Being told to be strong and courageous three times, then to have tacked on "Now remember Joshua, I said to be strong. And by the way now, don't be afraid or discouraged!" This is not rocket science you know. Anyone who has to give me a pep talk *repeatedly* must figure I actually need it. Do you have to tell your child not to eat a cookie *three times* unless she's already reaching for it?

Perhaps misery loves company, but I greatly appreciate the fact that God had to buck up even a Joshua for the daunting task that lay before him. It tells me there is nothing new under the sun. If a guy like Joshua had to overcome his fears, I guess God understands when I struggle with that as well.

For some reason, God felt the need to repeat himself *twice* to make sure Joshua got his point. God well knew that Joshua would have ample opportunity to be afraid, that he would have ample opportunity to be discouraged. Achieving the God-size destiny on his life was not going to be a cake walk. There would be suffering along the way. There could even be a momentary defeat (such as at Ai in the book of Joshua chapter eight), but if Joshua would stand courageous, God would see him through to the end. *He would not leave him alone.* As long as Joshua walked God's path, God was *always* there. Joshua's standing firm on God's promise that he would always be with him, consistently trumped the fear and discouragement twins.

And so it is with us. If our destiny did not have challenges associated with it, it would not be worth achieving. I suspect if we really could see what God has in mind for us, what we really could achieve for him, it would blow our collective minds and we would be wailing to go back to the comforts of Egypt. To achieve the God-size destiny we each have, we must remember who it is we are and that we are never alone. *He will never leave us or forsake us.* And the Lord is not surprised by our fear. He understands it, and that is why he doesn't leave us alone. Otherwise, we might be tempted to run. So message number one is this: even the heroes of faith felt fear, but they defeated it by continuing to step forward in trust.

You are Not Your Enemy's Biggest Problem

Here is the best part, and David made the interesting observation in another one of his psalms. "Lead me, O Lord, in Your righteousness because of *my* enemies . . . Pronounce them guilty, O God! Let them fall by their own counsels; cast them out in the multitude of their transgressions, for they have rebelled against *You*" (Ps. 5:8, 10, emphasis mine).

Why would David identify *his* enemies as being in rebellion against *God*? He understood that so long as we are walking God's path, so long as we are his humble and trusting servants, so long as we will fight the fight as instructed, then the enemies seeking to dislodge us from the destiny God has for our lives are not just *our* enemies but *God's* as well. The biggest problem they have to worry about is God, not us. God does not want either his plans or his people thwarted. That ought to add a new dynamism to our prayer lives as we pray to enforce the will of God for us. But enemies and opposition we will *always* have on this path.

Here is a thought: If we are not experiencing opposition to some degree, we should wonder if we are really on *God's* path. As Graham Cooke said in his message on *The Way of the Warrior*: "Crisis is a normal event on the road to our destiny. Crisis leads to elevation and will attract the power and strength of God. 'My grace is sufficient for you, My power is made perfect in weakness' (2 Cor. 12:9). . . . There can be no warfare without the majesty of God."

Cooke went on to quote a couple of key verses among others: "My brethren, count it all joy when you fall into various trials, knowing that the testing of your faith produces patience. But let patience have its perfect work, that you may be perfect and complete, lacking nothing" (James 1:2–4). "For in the time of trouble, He shall hide me in His pavilion; in the secret place of His tabernacle He shall hide me; He shall set me high upon a rock" (Ps. 27:5).

Defeat is but a pit stop on the road to God's destiny for us. What do we do in the face of it? We dare to praise him. What do we do in the face of suffering? We dare to praise him. What do we do in the face of obstacles on our path to God's destiny for our lives? We have the holy audacity to declare, "Though He slay me, yet will I trust Him" (Job 13:15).

I know this is not exactly what many Christians want to hear. I understand and respect that. The last thing anyone needs is me with pom-poms acting the cheerleader. Many are tired from the battle. Some have experienced great tragedy. Some have not entered into battle such as this, and they wonder why on earth anyone would be crazy enough to volunteer to do such a thing. Praise God after a major loss? Life is warfare? That doesn't sound enticing.

A reader might be asking, "Weren't things easier when I was just 'saved and safe,' doing my own thing, going to church every now and then?" The truth is that adversity, loss, and defeat are common life experiences. What's more, God has a different perspective on them than do we. We see them almost universally as bad, but God sees them as building blocks of our character on the road to our destiny. How we deal with these experiences and whether we turn them to our advantage, however, is a choice. Living in defeat is a choice. Turning defeat into a rung on the ladder to God's destiny for our lives is also a choice. God's will is *not* about defeat; it is about *victory*. We turn what the enemy meant for evil into victory by declaring the purposes of God into our circumstance.

Message number two is this: Our enemies are God's enemies. God's goal is to see us achieve the highest destiny he has for us. Only we can circumvent that by opting out of the process or succumbing to the lies of the Enemy, whose goal is to keep believers from God's best. Whereas this journey is not for the faint of heart, it is all about heart and how we must not lose it. It is all about overcoming the giants in our lives and recognizing that if we will but close our eyes and step out in faith, God will take us one more step into our destiny.

It was probably no accident that I found myself bored one recent Saturday night, and so I managed to catch the classic movie *Twelve O'clock High* on television. It was about American bomber pilots in World War II and all their emotional struggles under the great strain of warfare. In the old film footage of battle, the flak grew thickest the closer the plane got to its target. While the opportunity for fear was at its greatest, so was the greatest opportunity for victory.

As I reflect on the writing of this book, I have wondered at times if a piece of why God allowed my removal from office was in order to actually *qualify* me to write this. Knowing the Lord, I would not put it past him. It is an easy thing to say some of the things I have said from a position of having always won or having never experienced great adversity. It is quite another to be excited about God coming away from a place of loss and defeat. But I am excited. Sure, I have days like everybody else. Every day is not just one big smiley face. In the early aftermath of leaving office, there were mornings I had to make great effort to focus on my past in God just to get a grip on my future. Lori and I are not theoreticians. We are living it out day by day *just like everyone else*. I have shared some of our experiences, difficult as some have been, in order that you might take heart and be encouraged in an awesome and very real God. He is demonstrably faithful. The evidence of his faithfulness has been overwhelming to both of us. Even as that struggling, recovering skeptic, I now stand convicted of the reality of a supernatural life and no longer find it either wise or religiously fashionable to cling to the comfortable hopelessness that often permeates skepticism at its core. God loves us very much, and I stand in utter awe of how that *reality* has expressed itself in our life's experience.

The destiny and calling on your life is God-sized. If you knew what God actually had in mind, you might need as much bucking up as Joshua. God is in the business of being glorified. As his creation, we are here for the Creator's glory, not embarrassment. It greatly excites me to encourage my readers with the fact that God both wants and is highly motivated to help you live nothing less than an amazing, adventurous and victorious life. I pray that you step out and live exactly that. You will never, ever regret it.

CHAPTER TWELVE

A PASSAGE REMEMBERED

God has always been in the business of being glorified. If the artist of a beautiful painting deserves our praise and admiration, how much more the incomparable Creator of the universe? What is so extraordinary about God is that he loves us so much that one of the primary ways he likes to receive praise and admiration is through the lives of his children. Like any wonderful parent, he wants his children to stand out and to live lives of blessing and wonder and joy. He wants us to live a different life than anyone else—a supernatural life.

The long wooden conference table sitting in the DA library was marred and stained from its years of use, or perhaps misuse. It was probably already older than I was in 1988, but probably not older than the Korean man sitting across the table from me, his eyes nervously darting about the room avoiding contact with my own. He was scared. He needed to be. He was charged with murdering his wife and I was his prosecutor. He was wearing his jailhouse orange jumpsuit, complete with handcuffs. It was an unusual meeting as a prosecutor does not typically get together with a murder defendant for a chat before trial. Mr. Kim, however, was somehow different.

I had already visited the crime scene, just another apartment in another apartment house somewhere in town. It was there that the photos had depicted the dead Mrs. Kim, lying lifeless on her back upon a blood stained shag rug. Her eyes stared blankly, partially closed, partially revealing the whites in that weird, eerie way eyes stare when someone has been murdered. Of course, crime scene and autopsy photos were about the only pictures I ever saw of dead people, so how was I to know? Maybe they always do that when we're dead. Still, that "look" was rarely a peaceful one, more the look of a drunk, eyes lolling about without focus and then the snap of a photo captures them forever staring aimlessly into a stupor-filled void. But there was no confusing her with a drunk. Not with the rivulets of dried blood streaming across her cheeks as gravity brought them finally to the coagulated pool beneath her head. The small caliber bullet, as I recall, had penetrated her nose and entered her brain.

Now, some twenty years later, I don't remember how Mr. Kim's attorney convinced me to meet with his client. I just remember that I liked the lawyer and trusted him, and he was so very insistent that his client was innocent in that the gun had gone off accidentally. In any event, I agreed to meet with them.

The lawyer wanted his client to tell me personally exactly how it had all gone down, and how it was that I needed to believe Mr. Kim when he said that the gun's discharge had not been intentional. Mr. Kim's interpreter was the fourth person in the library with us. Although Kim did not speak much, if any, English, I'm not sure in retrospect he really even needed an interpreter because of the intensity that oozed off of him like sweat. He was wound very tight, his every movement intense and animated. His unintelligible words spilled out of him in a frantic, staccato beat, oddly offset by the calm demeanor of the interpreter's translation.

Today, in the vagaries of my memory, I do not recall what it was that convinced me he was telling the truth. Perhaps it was the desperation and plainly tearful fear. Perhaps it was that frantic and pleading demonstration of how the gun had accidently gone off. Nonetheless, it was supremely compelling. I pinned him down relentlessly on where he and Mrs. Kim were and where the gun's muzzle had been pointing exactly at the time it went off. He answered every question with the sad but rapid, solid assurance of an innocent man overwhelmed by the death of his beloved wife and the knowledge that her death, even by accident, had been at his hand.

I left the meeting knowing what I had to do. I immediately went to the office of the First Assistant District Attorney to tell him that I would not prosecute an innocent man. Pat Morgan, a crusty, retired Marine Corps Colonel from the Vietnam era, sat patiently behind the piles of books and files on his desk listening to me relate the meeting. He was second in command behind Mr. Macy, and he was the man who called me to offer me my prosecutor's job back a year or so before. He was one of my favorite people in the office and, although he would never admit it, I sensed he actually liked me, too. We had been on the same felony team several years before, not long before I left the office thinking I was going to be that rich trial lawyer. Our first meeting took place the day I walked into the empty office I was planning to move into. I really did not know much about him at the time, other than he was a retired Marine and was getting ready to graduate from law school. He was an intern in our office and, at that moment, was sitting at the desk I was planning to occupy.

"What are you doing here?" I asked.

"I thought I would take this office," he replied.

"Guess what? Me lawyer and you not," I cockily remarked. "Get out of my office."

I'm not sure the Colonel had ever been talked to like that, at least not since boot camp, and certainly not by anyone fifteen years or so his junior. But it was the beginning of beautiful relationship in so far as relationships go with crusty Marine Colonels and arrogant young prosecutors with more trial skill than good sense. By the time I had been humbled by life and returned to the DA's office, his leadership and administrative skill had quickly manifested itself during my four year absence and he was now my boss. It was an interesting turn of events.

After Morgan listened to my report of Mr. Kim's interview and my righteous pronouncement that I would not be party to such a prosecution, he looked at me through squinty eyes and a half smile and patiently told me to hang in the case for a bit longer and we would see how it shook out. He had not ordered me to try the case, but just to wait a bit longer. I left the office somehow mollified, at least for the moment.

It was not too much longer before I got the autopsy report back on Mrs. Kim clearly showing that Mr. Kim had lied through his teeth to me. The story he fabricated was physically impossible, considering the trajectory of the bullet wound and other details on which I had pinned him down during our meeting. I took him to trial, convicted him of first degree murder, and realized I learned a couple of important lessons from the Colonel through that experience. First, I couldn't tell worth a hoot if someone was lying to me, and second, that a wise man doesn't solely work off his feelings but waits to see the evidence of a matter. The wizened, battle-hardened Colonel knew what he was doing.

The Evidence of a Matter

On this the other side of my passage through the public eye, I have now had the opportunity to review the autopsy of my relationship with God through the crisp lens of hindsight. This being the case, I realize I would be remiss in this final chapter if I didn't share a critical piece of physical evidence God shared with me before taking office, and which would later help sustain me through some of the darker moments in that passage. That evidence came via the life of another man.

I first "met" George Müller in the mid 1980s, during what I call my "wilderness period," a time after my first marriage ended and when I languished in my misery as I tried to get a grip both on life and my fledgling relationship with God. Someone mentioned Müller and I checked out a biography on him from my church library. It was interesting and probably somewhat uplifting, but at that time it did not have much impact on me.

It was some ten years later, around 1996 or so that I once again found myself drawn to this man's life. I honestly don't recall what drew me back to him, but as I type this the thought popped into my mind that the Holy Spirit cannot be ruled out as the likely culprit.

My good friend, Jim Priest, dropped by the juvenile division one day to visit, and as he was leaving I found myself asking if he had ever heard of George Müller. Had he ever! Jim was a great fan of Müller and he later gave me a book that was to profoundly impact my life. The short little book by Roger Steer was entitled *Spiritual Secrets of George Müller.*[1] This book was made up primarily of Müller's experiences in his own words, drawn from the journals he kept over the some sixty years of his remarkable walk with God. These journals are entitled *Narratives of some of the Lord's dealings with George Müller.*[2] His life epitomized the supernatural walk with God.

For those who either disbelieve or doubt of God's existence, or those who view God in a highly limited fashion, I urge you to get to know George Müller. You can go online and read his journals. Müller was exacting proof that God not only exists, but that he is aggressively engaged in the lives of his kids. As a fellow who knows something about convicting evidence, the evidence is simply overwhelming.

A Simple Motive

Müller was born in Prussia in 1805, and after living the wild life as a very young man, became a Christian. He moved to England in 1829. It was his life's work in establishing and operating orphanages from 1836 until his death in 1898 that turned the Christian world of that era on its ear. What was of particular interest to me was his motivation for getting involved with orphans. A pastor by profession in Bristol, England, he found himself saddened that most Christians of that day did not believe the God of the Bible still moved in supernatural ways (sounds familiar today). Steer quotes Müller himself for his motivation for starting the orphanages.[3] This passage comes from his 1837 journal:

> Through my pastoral labors . . . I had constantly cases brought before me which proved that one of the especial things which the children of God needed in our day was to have their faith strengthened . . . There was no trust in God. No real belief in the truth of that word: *'Seek first the kingdom of God, and His righteousness and all these things shall be added unto you.'* I longed therefore to have something to point the brother to, as a visible proof that our God and Father is the same faithful God as ever He was; as willing as ever to prove Himself to be the living God in our day as formerly to all who put their trust in Him . . . very rarely

did I see that there was a stand made for God, that there was the holy determination to trust in the living God, and to depend on Him . . .

My spirit longed to be instrumental in strengthening their faith by giving them not only instances from the Word of God of His willingness and ability to help all those who rely upon Him, but to show them by proofs that He is the same in our day.

Now if I, a poor man, simply by prayer and faith, obtained, without asking any individual, the means for establishing and carrying on an orphan-house, there would be something which, with the Lord's blessing, might be instrumental in strengthening the faith of the children of God, besides being a testimony to consciences of the unconverted of the reality of the things of God.

This, then, was the primary reason for establishing the orphan-house.

The Two Hundred Million Dollar Man

From this point until his death, Müller built five orphanages, fed, clothed and housed thousands of orphans and supported ministries around the world. Those working for him knew they were never to tell anyone of their needs. It was forbidden. There were no fundraising banquets, no committees, and no mass mailings with financial appeals. Nothing. Even when he was specifically asked if they had need of anything he always declined to answer and would say something to the effect of "God is providing" or the like. In his journal he kept thousands of pages of meticulous records delineating his prayers and God's responses. *Any and all monies given to this ministry came solely through prayer and prayer alone.* His annual reports on God's responses to prayer transfixed his readers. Though not his goal, he became an international celebrity of sorts in the realm of the faithful.

And did the provision ever come. At the time of his death, the sixty years of detailed expenditures for the institution were added up (the expenditures being a reflection of what had been donated) and totaled *one and one-half million British pounds*, which in today's American dollars would be conservatively put at over *two hundred million!*[4] Sixty years of living by God's responses to believing prayers. Sixty years of walking out the supernatural life with God. Sixty years of proving God's faithfulness. It would be interesting to see what charities today with a multi-decade history would even come close to this success, even with the most aggressive and overt fundraising campaigns.

The evidence of this man's supernatural life's experience was incontrovertible, and what was particularly encouraging was Müller's emphasis on the fact that he was nothing unique or special. That may sound strange to say, because as I talk to other Christians so many of us have a tendency to look upon Müller's life with a certain awe and reverence. We take on a point of view that somehow he *was* special, and that somehow his life was uniquely designed and reserved by God for George Müller and no one else. But all he really ever did was simply follow the prescription given by the Bible for walking out the supernatural life. He did this by making the decision to take God at his Word and *believe* that when God said to seek him first then all the rest would be added (Matt. 6:33[5]). He believed God indeed meant what he said. Any "uniqueness" or "specialness" in Müller comes solely from the fact that he was fearless in stepping out on faith. The vast bulk of Christians are intimidated at the thought of doing that, and I know the finger points at me as well as anyone. So very, very few of us are actually willing to step out and test God's promises.

Winging God

I went to lunch one day with a pastor visiting from Africa, a jovial, unpretentious man, who in his small village was experiencing marvelous miracles of healing. He was not a seminary trained pastor or someone who had a faith inspiring vision of Jesus commanding him to pray for people's healing. Nothing like that. I asked him how it was he decided to start praying for healing among his people. He smiled, shrugged his shoulders, and in his heavily accented English responded, "I read the first six chapters of the gospel of Mark and decided to give it a try!" This man simply took God at his word. It sent chills up and down my anal-retentive core. The very thought of reading a few chapters of the

173

Bible and then just *winging it* blew my mind. Yet, honestly, that was pretty much what Jesus had his disciples doing. He demonstrated what he wanted done, gave a couple of sentences worth of instructions, and then shipped the disciples out. No theological seminary or divinity school, no how-to manual with pictures, no teaching tapes—nothing. The only thing they really needed to drag along with them was the simple belief that God would actually follow through as promised.

Our Walk, Our Choice

It seems to me there are two different walks through life. At least these are the two walks I have taken. On one end of the spectrum is the natural walk. This walk through life is directed by luck and common sense. Those pursuing the natural walk are individuals who claim *no* relationship with Christ. It is also the walk taken by many carnal Christians who have accepted Christ as their savior, but these family members have pretty much moved out of the house to live on their own. (I realize there is an argument here that someone like this might not have truly had a conversion experience in the first place, but I'll leave that to the theologians to debate and for God to decide.)

For example, just because I am a "Lane" doesn't mean I have to have anything to do with my family. When I was twenty-six years old I did not necessarily *have to* listen to my mother or father's advice on living, or anyone else's for that matter (and I didn't, I might add). I did what I wanted to do. Perhaps I was just expressing my independence, or maybe I was in rebellion. I didn't "salute" anyone in authority over me, unless it suited me. I listened to no one and didn't care about anyone's interests other than my own. I had no real interaction with the family of God. Thus, whether technically "Christian" or not, my life was directed by me, my luck, and my common sense. My walk was in the "natural."

The second walk is a bit more complicated because there are different "trails" we can take as we exercise our free will within a framework of God directing our lives (as opposed to us directing our own lives as in the natural experience). This walk is in the "super-natural." How much of God we want to experience, or what trails we take, is going to largely be a matter of our personal decision.

Perhaps this might be helpful. When I finally committed my life to Christ in my late twenties, I was at a point I no longer even wanted to attempt directing my life any longer, I had so botched things. I desperately wanted God to direct things from there on out. I was finally taking God's path and, as if through an amazing forest, my Guide (God) started me out on trails I could handle. It was not long before I was given opportunities to take steeper trails, trails that were tougher and required me to have a greater vision of God and his willingness to take care of me. These steeper trails developed in me a greater faith in a supernatural God and what he was willing to do in my life. My Guide loved me so much that he was patient when I chose an easier trail, but he kept presenting me with the more difficult terrain.

I discovered the steeper terrain was even somewhat painful because the trails were mountainous and rocky. But the vistas, once reached, were breathtaking and far superior to that which I had been willing to settle for on other paths. These vistas were so marvelous that I became all the more determined to keep walking the path and God was willing to lead me to as many vistas as my faith could handle. My Guide was also loving and patient with me when my doubts and fears drove me to stop and camp for a period—although I'd like to ask him someday if my "camping" might have hurt his feelings a wee bit since it was a clear statement that I would not trust his leadership.

Opting Out of God's Best

Every step of this walk is a choice for us. We can have as much of God as we can handle. Even the nation of Israel decided to give in to fear and let God know that they only wanted so much of him. After seeing the fireworks of God when Moses visited him on Mount Sinai to receive the Ten Commandments, they were content to stay a good distance from the mountain and let Moses be their intermediary.[6] They chose to limit their God experience and God honored their unfortunate decision.

Moses, on the other hand, got to enjoy a far more amazing path than the others when God was apparently willing to give the entire nation a much richer relationship. The same applies to us as committed believers today. We love God, but often we are content to remain a safe distance from the mountain. We choose to experience the Lord from

175

a distance, to hear the rumble of his voice, but not receive the power of his presence. We are content to let others relate wondrous stories of God's intervention, but for whatever reason are not willing to reach out and grab the supernatural for ourselves.

For a multitude of reasons, this is where a great number of Christians "opt out" of the supernatural life. Like Jesus' "Parable of the Sower,"[7] many hear the word of God and have the opportunity to walk an amazing walk, but the reality is that few take advantage of it. The first line of Rick Warren's *The Purpose Driven Life* says "It's not about you."[8] Warren's point is that our life is about God, not ourselves, but that has always been the problem. We Americans are overtly self-focused and usually uninterested in the rigorous course of God's faith development plan. We as American Christians are far more likely to have a fast food faith mentality in our walks with God. We want it our way and we want it now. As author Dutch Sheets said, "We are into microwaving and God is more into marinating."[9]

Small wonder why there appears to be scant difference in the quality of lives lived by those with absolutely no relationship with Jesus at all as compared to many who claim to love him. Why else do we think, for example, that the incidence of divorce in the church is about the same rate as those who claim no faith in Christ at all? Skeptics point to this situation as being evidence that walking with Jesus has no real power. But the truth is, it is only evidence that we can claim Jesus but choose not to live in the fullness of the Christian experience. Having been there and done that, I would suggest it is not that God's rules for marriage don't work, but rather it is that we as Jesus-followers are not working the rules.

At times, we are all form but little substance, single dimension Christian cardboard cutouts. It is sad that in many cases *we really don't want to be* like this at all. Yet, it is our choice to opt out of God's best. In the end, too many of us quote a verse that does not even exist in Scripture: "God helps those who help themselves." And we delude ourselves in the belief that living the theme of Frank Sinatra's song "My Way" is actually somehow consistent with life God's way. Even though we really do believe in God and even though we do attend church, our lives are little different from those who haven't a clue about

Jesus Christ or for what the gospel means. Tony Campolo addressed a large church and commented on the self-focused and ineffective lives of many Christians by saying, "You people come to church, sing a thousand verses of 'Just as I Am,' and you leave just as you were."

Grabbing for All the Gusto

George Müller lived an amazing, supernatural life with God because he decided he would reach out and grab it. He understood it would be painful but that if he was willing to go the distance, God's wonder would permeate every aspect of his being; that every little thing would be brought under the lordship of Jesus. It was not just money, but every need, every decision, and every relationship.[10] As stated earlier, Müller was quite adamant about his not having the "gift of faith" as found in 1 Corinthians chapter twelve. He didn't get a special "leg up" on the situation from God. He *chose* to work the rules; to keep taking the steeper paths, and as a result, he got the privilege of viewing the greater vistas. As he told a Reverend Sawtell about faith:

> The first germ of faith in the soul is very much like a new-born infant in the cradle, very small and very weak, and its future growth and increase of strength as much depend on its daily constant exercise, as does the physical development of the child; yes, I can now as easily trust God for thirty-five thousand pounds as I could at first for five thousand.[11]

What Jesus did at the cross was costly. Anything really worth having has its price. Not everyone is willing to pay, for the cost may be more than many can bear. It is simply not an easy journey. Maybe I can now run a spiritual marathon, but there was a lot of throwing up along the way. The grander the vistas on the supernatural path, the greater the cost. It does, however, make life worth living. As they say, "misery loves company," and I confess to being encouraged that even the great George Müller struggled:

> Let no one ascribe to George Müller such a miraculous gift of faith as lifted him above common believers and out of the reach of the temptations and infirmities to which all

fallible souls are exposed. He was constantly liable to satanic assaults, and we find him making frequent confession of the same sins as others, and even of unbelief and at times overwhelmed with the genuine sorrow for his departures from God. In fact, he felt himself rather more than usually wicked by nature, and utterly helpless even as a believer.[12]

Biographer Arthur T. Pierson went on to point out that it was Müller's recognition of his own weakness and ability that drove his utter dependence upon God and which resulted in his abiding prayer life. And, having run the race, Müller could reflect on an amazing God to Pierson not long before his death: "Not once, or five times, or five hundred times, but thousands of times in these threescore years, have we had in hand enough *for one more meal*, either in food or in funds; but not once has God failed us; not once have we or the orphans gone hungry or lacked any good thing."[13]

We have the opportunity to experience a walk with God that is beyond the normal, one directed by God on a trail constantly marked by the influence of a loving, interested, and involved heavenly Father. It is a walk that contemplates the destiny he has for our lives and the interaction we have with him in achieving that end. It is the life marked by prayer and a relationship committed to conversation with a living and supernatural being. It is about achieving intimacy with the King of the universe. Many Christians today are *not* experiencing this kind of harmonic and victorious life. Their lives are largely indistinguishable from those who do not know or love God; lives that are far less than what he wants for all his children. That is absolutely *not* God's desire. Jesus said he came that we might have the *abundant* life.[14] Many of us are settling for the bargain basement spiritual life. I know I certainly have at times.

The Non-Negotiables

I cannot over-emphasize the subject of prayer. It is simply *everything*. Prayer and obedience are two non-negotiables for intimacy with God. I suppose in some respects when it gets right down to it, we probably aren't going to have much prayer going on if our attitude—our obedience—is not right in the first place. When I was a kid, I tended to avoid my dad for the most part when I was disinclined to follow his instructions. Our conversations were limited to my surly grunts at the breakfast table and, not surprisingly, he was certainly in no mood to bless me. Suffice it to say, our attitude flows into our prayer life and it will be the ultimate determining factor concerning our living out the supernatural walk of God. Prayer is a reflection of our attitude, our "heart." Here are a few thoughts on prayer that might be helpful:

- Prayer is moving from the plane of living by common sense to living on the supernatural level—Oswald Chambers

- Prayer is not a program but a dependent relationship upon God through which we are empowered and filled by His Holy Spirit—John Devries

- Prayer is the atmosphere within which we walk our lives—George Kouri

- Prayer begins with the realization that I am loved by God as I am. God's love is based on nothing and, therefore, is the most basic and secure fact in my life. I simply let myself be loved by God. This is not so much an activity of mine but a passivity in which I let God's love soak in and permeate my whole being.—Peter Van Breeman, S.J.

I especially like Kouri's thought because it takes into account a sort of completeness, a totality, the very air we breathe. Everything we do, everything we touch and everything we represent exists within a framework of the relationship we have with God. The supernatural life could likewise be said to be the atmosphere within which we exist.

Some people consider the term supernatural as being just the occasional miraculous event. But it is so much more. It is miraculous because it is God, but it is not just an event. It is a lifestyle through which God is constantly being glorified through our very lives day in and day out. He is not glorified when we as Christians choose to live natural lives no different from anyone else. When we largely mimic an unbelieving world, we only dumb down what God has for us.

Why Our Prayers Matter

There was a time in my life that I honestly wondered, *what is the point of prayer?* It just seemed like all I was doing was hurling noise into the atmosphere. Was anybody really listening? I have already shared the event that radically changed my mind on this, the Crystal Dittmeyer case, but it wasn't until I read Dutch Sheets's marvelous book *Intercessory Prayer*[15] that I finally understood why our prayers really matter and how critical a role we play in the development of God's will on the earth. In short, it is the system God set up at the earth's creation to give humans dominion over the earth and a responsibility for earth's caretaking. It was Jesus himself who told us to pray: ". . . Your kingdom come, Your will be done, on earth as it is in Heaven" (Luke 11:2).

So what is the significance of Jesus' instruction?

Prayer was Jesus' primary ministry. I believe it was Larry Lea who once said that Jesus went from one prayer meeting with God to the next, performing miracles between the meetings! He was our role model for living out the supernatural life with God by modeling dependence upon God through prayer. God had a plan for Jesus and it required the Savior—of all people—to pray that the Father's will would be released upon the earth. If Jesus depended upon prayer, surely we must as well. Because the divine will is not always automatic, it is our responsibility to pray that God's will in heaven would prevail on the earth. We are God's ambassadors on this planet, and the way we enforce God's will is through our prayer. God's designs for the world are not all set on auto-pilot. Jesus understood that all those walking out the supernatural life must understand we have a role to play in the system God established from the beginning. This was something George Müller understood very well. Our prayers are critical. We matter.

Dutch Sheets said that, "Prayer does more than just motivate the Father to action; it releases the power of the Holy Spirit from us to accomplish things." When we pray, we are pushing back darkness. We enforce the work Jesus did legally at the cross.[16] We pray that God's will in heaven be enforced upon the earth against those demonic beings who insist on clinging to lost ground, ground they no longer legally occupy, ground upon which they trespass. This ground may constitute one's family or one's career or one's well-being. We have authority to pray to enforce this under a system God *chose* to set up. But an enemy does not volunteer to return that which he stole. These are matters of spiritual warfare, and like it or not, that requires a fight. Jesus said that "from the days of John the Baptist until now the kingdom of heaven suffers violence, and the violent take it by force" (Matt. 11:12).

Remember, even when God *gave* Israel the Promised Land, they still had to *fight* for it. Christianity is not a spectator sport.

A Path Worth Walking

I realize this "spiritual warfare" talk may seem somewhat daunting, all this praying and fighting and adversity and the like. It sounds as though I am just trying to get you to sign up for one more thing you have to check off of your list. We are already harried at work and at home, and everyone clamors for our attention. For all the devices that are supposedly designed to make our lives easier, doesn't it seem that life has become more complicated? Life on the prairie about a hundred years ago has, at times, carried a certain attraction to my mind. For one thing, I certainly would not receive any of those supposedly cute, "you've gotta read this" e-mails that are forwarded around about a million times.

But the greatest life simplification device ever created is the super-natural life. We will never escape adversity, no matter what we do or what we trim back. However, if there is a *superior* experience, an abundant life available even in the midst of adversity and distraction, why would most of us settle for an inferior experience?

Fighting the Good Fight

In the fall of 2007, I was at home in my den, typing away on this book when I felt the slightest impression that I needed to stop what I was doing and pray for Lori's safety—right then and there. It was so very subtle. Lori went to visit her father in Wichita, Kansas, and was driving home that night. I stopped my typing and got on my knees (it seemed to be a knee moment) and began praying a hedge of protection around Lori, praying that any assignment of harm against my wife be broken in Jesus name. I continued praying a warfare kind of prayer

181

for a few minutes, and then I felt it was time to quit. I returned to my computer. Some fifteen minutes later Lori showed up in the doorway with the words excitedly tumbling out of her mouth about how she had just very nearly had a high speed collision on I-35! It was dark and as she was changing lanes to turn off the highway, she had not seen an Oklahoma City police car coming barreling at high speed down the lane into which she was going (the patrol car had no overhead lights on, which is standard procedure on highways as it is often more distracting to other drivers to race by with flashing lights). Both Lori's car and the police car went fishtailing about to avoid careening into one another. The patrol car ended up stopping Lori and the officer was obviously just as terrified from the experience as was Lori (no, she did not get a ticket). I asked Lori when this had happened. All of this took place at the exact same period during which I had been on my knees praying for her protection.

That, my friends, is the *supernatural* life. That is the life God wants for *you*. It is the atmosphere within which we are meant to live. As I said of George Müller earlier, I say about me: There is nothing unique or special about either of us, but God wants us *all* to walk in this way. It is simply a choice we have to decide to make.

God has a plan that is wonderful for each of us. It involves great joy and fulfillment, even in the midst of terrible suffering. It is a peace even on the high seas of travail. It involves Christ's supernatural power backing us up, and because it involves his being glorified, it is more than we could possibly imagine. God's plan is simply the best. It requires us, however, to let go and stop chasing what we *think* is important and follow the path God *knows* is important.

Twenty plus years ago I had utterly failed. Life was not working out as I had planned. At last I realized it was time to jettison my plan. Perhaps you have been there. Perhaps you are there right now. If so, then I am very excited for you, because if you decide to give up *your* plan and start working *His*, you will be embarking on a great and exciting adventure. You will never regret leaving an inferior life experience. Today, the ocean may be roiling around Lori and me, our ship may be tossed about, but Jesus indeed has provided us an abundant life, a life he has planned, a supernatural experience that has made every steep trail worth it—so much so that we find ourselves seeking the next amazing vista. The Lord is *supernaturally* in the midst of our every circumstance. There is no chaos in Christ.

I believe, given a real glimpse of just what God has to offer, that most of us would want a superior experience in life. The evidence is very clear. There are too many people out there who have seen the vistas and reported them for such views not to be available to all. That has been our experience. We have been fortunate to have had others beckon us on from farther up the trail. We are beginning to experience what we could only once observe from a distance. By sharing a small portion of our own life's experience, I hope and pray that in some small way I am doing that for you now, that I am beckoning you farther up the trail. God is indeed a rewarder of those who diligently pursue him.[17] The King of the universe is actually eager to have his heart moved by our believing prayers. As in the following vignette of George Müller and a ship's captain, lives will be transformed by God's responses to our believing prayers.[18]

The Müllers set off for the United States in August 1877 aboard the 4,000 ton ship the Sardinian. For some reason they had been allocated the chief officer's deck room for their cabin, which Susannah [Mrs. Müller] found to be "tolerably comfortable." Although the Atlantic was rough, the ship remained on schedule until running into thick fog off Newfoundland. Captain Dutton had been on the bridge for twenty-four hours when George Müller appeared at his side.

"Captain, I have come to tell you that I must be in Quebec by Saturday afternoon."

"It is impossible," said the captain.

"Very well," said Müller, "if your ship cannot take me, God will find some other way. I have never broken an engagement in fifty-two years. Let us go down into the chart-room and pray."

Captain Dutton wondered which lunatic asylum Müller had escaped from.

"Mr. Müller," he said, "do you know how dense this fog is?"

"No, my eye is not on the density of the fog, but on the living God who controls every circumstance of my life."

Müller then knelt down and prayed simply. When he had finished, the captain was about to pray, but Müller put his hand on his shoulder.

"Do not pray. First, you don't believe He will answer; and second, I believe He has and there is no need whatever for you to pray about it."

Captain Dutton looked at Müller in amazement.

"Captain," Müller continued, "I have known my Lord for fifty-two years, and there has never been a single day that I have failed to get an audience with the King. Get up, Captain, and open the door, and you will find the fog is gone."

The captain walked across to the door and opened it. The fog had lifted.

Captain Dutton retold the story many times as master of the Sardinian; a well-known nineteenth century evangelist subsequently described him as "one of the most devoted men I ever knew."

May your passage through life be all that God has planned for you. May you never settle for anything less.

Call to Me and I will answer you and I will tell you great and mighty things which you do not know.

—Jeremiah 33:3

EPILOGUE

This book has in part been about the development of "salt and light leadership." The role of such Christian leadership has been further developed and implemented in a program created by Wes Lane, The Burbridge Foundation, and a group of dedicated Christian leaders called "S.A.L.L.T."—*Salt and Light Leadership Training*. For more information on how you can be a salt and light leader, go to www. saltandlightleadership.com.

ENDNOTES

Chapter Two: I Think I Am in Love with Me

1. Merriam-Webster's® 11th Collegiate Dictionary (Springfield, Mass.: G&C Merriam Company, 2003).
2. 2 Corinthians 6:14
3. I almost refrain from sharing this very brief vignette because this book is not about my dating life. It is, however, about life with God, and part of that is the especially youthful focus of seeking a mate and God's willingness to see to it we get the one he has in mind.
4. Lori was, in many ways, an instrument of God's saving me from myself. She literally saved me from financial ruin as a young man. It is no small fact that the governor would never have appointed me District Attorney in 2001 had I been forced into bankruptcy over my early years of financial foolishness. This, in itself, is a striking example of God's promise in Hebrews 11:6 that he rewards those who diligently seek him. He graciously paved the way for this later assignment. God has a plan for you as well.

Chapter Three: Who You Gonna Believe? Me, or Your Lyin' Eyes?

1. At the time of this writing, the nationally syndicated television program *Forensic Files* still airs a program about this case. The

Canadian *Discovery Channel* and *NBC Dateline* have also aired programs dedicated to the Hamilton case.

2. Assistant District Attorney Connie Smotherman tried the case with me and Oklahoma City Police Detectives Randy Scott (the lead investigator for the case) and Theresa Sterling sat as case agents.

Chapter Four: The Payoff of Pursuit

1. The case was State v. Gary Lee Rawlings. The detective who solved it was Oklahoma City Police homicide detective Larry Andrews, who would later become my dear friend, brother in the Lord, and Chief Investigator when I became District Attorney. An international case in the recent spotlight concerns the missing British child, Madeleine McCann. Her parents have at one time been viewed as suspects by the Portuguese authorities but their chief prosecutor refuses to prosecute without her body being found. He told *24 Horas* newspaper that "without the little girl's body, everything is extremely complicated. There have been cases where it is possible to obtain a conviction without there being a victim, but there were confessions."

2. This presentation was on audiotape from www.grahamcooke.com.

3. Husbands, if you are not praying with your wives you are missing out on a profound spiritual experience. My journal entry perhaps best expresses my personal experience:

> **Journal: Monday, August 23, 1999**
>
> I am so grateful to God. Not for any one thing; it is more global this morning. It is difficult to express what he is doing with Lori and me just now. I can only time it back to the point we starting praying together routinely every evening, on our knees before God, asking fervently that we might experience him fully, that he would hold nothing back from us, and that we might have relationship "to the max" with him. The level of our emotional intimacy has skyrocketed. I felt Lori's respect before this time, but even now there would seem to be no comparison. Whereas Lori was originally reluctant to have one more thing "on her plate" by having to pray together, it has become a time

of profound relationship. Whereas she, being intimidated in having to "perform" in front of others (including me at times), in this case by praying aloud our prayers are now becoming more conversational—and Lori is the one who has been interjecting!

4. Psalm 22:3
5. Psalm 89:14

Chapter Five: Spilling the Beans

1. Memphis, Tenn. The Master Design, 1999.
2. "If I regard iniquity in my heart, the Lord will not hear" (Ps. 66:18).
3. Frizzell, 58. The author also states a profound truth when he says in his Introduction, "No one's relationship with Christ will ever rise above the level of his or her praying."
4. "But God forbid that I should boast except in the cross of our Lord Jesus Christ, by whom the world has been crucified to me, and I to the world" (Gal. 6:14).
5. 1 Samuel 17:26
6. The *Pentateuch* or *Torah* is the most sacred of Hebrew writings and is comprised of what is known in the first five books of the Christian Old Testament as Genesis, Exodus, Leviticus, Numbers and Deuteronomy.
7. "Death and life are in the power of the tongue, and those who love it will eat its fruit" (Prov. 18:21).
8. It is noteworthy that David himself uses the word "lovingkindness" in his psalm of repentance for his actions concerning Bathsheba: "Have mercy upon me, O God, according to Your lovingkindness; according to the multitude of Your tender mercies, blot out my transgressions, wash me thoroughly from my iniquity, and cleanse me from my sin" (Ps. 51:1–2).
9. "[I] do not cease to give thanks for you, making mention of you in my prayers: that the God of our Lord Jesus Christ, the Father of glory, may give to you the spirit of wisdom and revelation in the knowledge of Him, the eyes of your understanding being enlightened; that you may know what is the hope of His calling, what are the riches of the glory of His inheritance in the saints, and what

is the exceeding greatness of His power toward us who believe, according to the working of His mighty power" (Eph. 1:16–19).

Chapter Six: That's *Mister* Head Honcho to You, Pal

1. Francis Frangipane, *Holiness, Truth and the Presence of God* (Cedar Rapids, IA.: Arrow Publications, 1986), 109.
2. Hugh Hewitt, *The Embarrassed Believer* (Nashville: Word Publishing, 1998).
3. The story of David dancing before the ark is found in 2 Samuel chapter 6.

Chapter Seven: Healed

1. "If you keep My commandments, you will abide in My love, just as I have kept My Father's commandments and abide in His love. These things I have spoken to you, that My joy may remain in you, and that your joy may be full" (John 15:10–11).
2. "Behold, I give you the authority to trample on serpents and scorpions and over all the power of the enemy and nothing shall by any means hurt you" (Luke 10:19).
3. Larry Lea's book *The Weapons of Your Warfare* comes to mind (Carol Stream, Ill.: Creation House, 1989).
4. Sweeps week is the period during which a television station gauges its audience share for the purpose of determining how much they can charge advertisers. They generally work to have exciting stories to encourage bigger audience viewing during that period.
5. Honesty is *always* the best policy. It was by being honest in filling out the licensure form's question on whether she had ever had treatment for a drug or alcohol issue over the preceding year that triggered an investigation by the Oklahoma Bureau of Narcotics. To have lied on the form would certainly have avoided Lori's prospective legal problems, but at what spiritual cost? It was this entire process that ultimately resulted in a profound answer to our longstanding prayer that Lori might experience the promised joy.

Chapter Nine: The Headwinds of Responsibility (State of Oklahoma v. Terry Lynn Nichols)

1. Charles Colson, *Born Again* (Grand Rapids: Chosen Books Inc., 1976).
2. Dietrich Bonhoeffer, *The Cost of Discipleship* Dietrich Bonhoeffer (New York: The MacMillan Company, 1959).
3. Going to this man to seek his forgiveness was doubtless one of the hardest things I have ever done. The theft had taken place a decade earlier while I was still in college. No one knew I had done this. Yet again, it was John Dwyer who first started sharing how he was making amends on some of his more unsavory collegiate activities and began urging me to do the same out of obedience to our new Boss—God. In my misery, I finally confessed my deed to my fairly new wife, Lori, who immediately echoed John in where my duty as a Christian lay. In an unbelievable state of dread, I mailed the man a check to more than cover what I had taken. Then, a few days later I called him to ask if I could come see him and explain why I sent him the money. Lori went with me. It was an incredible meeting during which I shared my faith as my motivation for seeking him out and during which he forgave me for my wronging him. I left his home feeling the great weight of my guilt lifted and all closet skeletons removed. Years later, before I became DA, I ran into him again, at which time he told me that if I ever wanted to run for DA, he wanted to hold a fundraising party for me! A gracious and forgiving man and a remarkable example of God's loving regard for obedience.
4. Judson Cornwall, *Praying the Scriptures* (Lake Mary, Fla.: Creation House, 1988).

Chapter Ten: Countering Culture

1. This concept permeates the New Testament. For example, see Philippians 2:5–8.
2. Matthew 23:27
3. "Do not think that I came to bring peace on earth. I did not come to bring peace but a sword. For I have come to set a man against

his father, a daughter against her mother, and a daughter-in-law against her mother-in-law; and a man's enemies will be those of his own household" (Matt. 10:34–36).

4. "For this purpose the Son of God was manifested, that He might destroy the works of the devil" (1 John 3:8).

5. "O My Father, if it is possible, let this cup pass from Me; nevertheless, not as I will, but as You will" (Matt. 26:39).

6. John 10:10

7. "And Jabez called on the God of Israel saying, 'Oh, that You would bless me indeed, and enlarge my territory, that Your hand would be with me, and that You would keep me from evil, that I may not cause pain!' So God granted him what he requested" (1 Chron. 4:10).

8. See Matthew 10:35–36

Chapter Eleven: Defeat and Destiny

1. Lewis Carroll, *Alice's Adventures in Wonderland*, various editions.

2. Psalm 119:105

3. Controversy over the bombing case was light fare compared to the rumors and tales being spread about. Some were test driven over the first year of my being in office and throughout that hot summer of election year 2002. One popular rumor being spread in that election was that Lori was arrested for driving drunk and that I, being the evil fellow I was, had covered the whole thing up with the police! I once confronted a criminal defense lawyer I learned was spreading around this nasty and malicious rumor. I was naively shocked to observe that not only did he not deny spreading the lie, but in fact was completely unembarrassed about doing so. Welcome to politics—for that matter, welcome to life!

4. Harry S. Truman

5. 1 Thessalonians 5:17

6. There is no criticism whatsoever intended for the Oklahoma Court of Appeals in their decision in the Crider case. I do not infer a demonic influence upon the court in their decision. Many things influence us, Satan being but one. As much as any influence would arise from the fact that a majority of the court is reputed to have

a "liberal" as opposed to "conservative" point of view. As I have expressed herein and again to borrow from Harry Truman, the buck stops solely with me.

7. 1 Timothy 6:12
8. John 10:10
9. "So I sought for a man among them who would make a wall, and stand in the gap before Me on behalf of the land, that I should not destroy it; but I found no one" (Ezek. 22:30).
10. See Joshua 4:1–9
11. The Oklahoma City Police Lab was under fire because of allegations that its one time director falsified lab findings in an effort to please the Oklahoma County District Attorney's office under Bob Macy. This was the reason why some were calling for the next district attorney to come from outside the office in order to avoid the taint of scandal.

Chapter Twelve: A Passage Remembered

1. Roger Steer, *Spiritual Secrets of George Müller* (Carol Stream, Ill. Harold Shaw Publishers, 1985). Sadly, this book is no longer in print, but a bit of searching on the internet might locate a used copy.
2. In tribute to Müller, I entitled my spiritual journal similarly "Journal of the Lord's dealings with Wes Lane." Müller, however, was far and away a more meticulous journalist than I have found myself to be.
3. Steer, 13.
4. The value of 1.0 pounds in 1898 money would in 2006 have a value of 76.58 pounds. Müller received almost 1.5 million pounds over his ministry life. The 2006 exchange rate pound/dollar is $1.84 to the pound. The value of 1.5 million pounds in 1898 would today be 114,870,000 pounds or $211,360,800. This is a very conservative figure considering we are only calculating the value since 1898, the end of Müller's ministry. There certainly would have also been an inflated monetary value over the sixty plus years Müller asked only God for his financial provision. Source: www.measuringworth.com.

5. "But seek first the kingdom of God and His righteousness, and all these things shall be added to you" (Matt. 6:33).

6. "Now all the people witnessed the thundering, the lighting flashes, the sound of the trumpet, and the mountain smoking; and when the people saw it, they trembled and stood afar off. Then they said to Moses, 'You speak with us, and we will hear; but let not God speak with us, lest we die'" (Ex. 20:18–19).

7. "Therefore hear the parable of the sower: When anyone hears the word of the kingdom, and does not understand it, then the wicked one comes and snatches away what was sown in his heart. This is he who received the seed by the wayside. But he who received the seed on stony places, this is he who hears the word and immediately receives it with joy; yet he has no root in himself, but endures only for a while. For when tribulation or persecution arises because of the word, immediately he stumbles. Now he who received seed among the thorns is he who hears the word, and the cares of this world and the deceitfulness of riches choke the work, and he becomes unfruitful. But he who received seed on the good ground is he who hears the word and understands it, who indeed bears fruit and produces: some a hundredfold, some sixty, some thirty" (Matt. 13:18–23).

8. Rick Warren, *The Purpose Driven Life* (Grand Rapids: Zondervan Publishing House, 2002).

9. Dutch Sheets, *Intercessory Prayer* (Ventura, Calif.: Regal Books, 1996), 17.

10. Müller also spoke on the point that there was nothing too small for God's attention. That being something I have observed about God, I include a small episode from my journal:

> **Journal: Tuesday, August 15, 2000**
>
> It's 4:30 a.m. and I am sitting in my "easy chair" in the den. Ralph [our Bassett/Beagle] is in his customary position on the sofa with his head buried beneath one of the big pillows. The box fan is running to hopefully drown out his snoring.

I suppose I should continue in the vein of the Lord's dealings in my life, but first an interesting anecdote of how God is interested in answering even the most trivial of prayer: A couple of months or so ago we got a new puppy. This new puppy, an Italian Greyhound Lori has named Gnocchi (meaning "little dumpling") was definitely unwelcome with Ralph. Her tiny body would chase him all over creation. It was patent that he could not stand her and in fact was clearly depressed over this new addition. So depressed that Lori even wanted me to speak to the vet concerning having him put on doggie anti-depressants! It was also a great pain in the rear to us because we had to cordon off areas to keep them away from one another. Ralph wouldn't bite her, although I encouraged him to do so if she would leave him alone. This went on for weeks and was really quite a problem, so much so that Lori and I decided one night to actually pray about the dog situation, pray for Ralph's depression, pray that the darn things would just get along!

So that night, perhaps three weeks ago, we prayed. Literally, the very next morning Lori calls me. It seems that Ralph and Gnocchi are having a high time chasing one another about the house! An unheard of event! Up to that moment it had always been Gnocchi driving Ralph crazy and causing him to jump up on furniture to get out of her path. That night I witnessed the change myself. Indeed, there they were just having a great time, one chasing the other, then reversing course and the other giving chase! And it has never stopped. In fact a couple of Saturdays ago I was in my chair with both dogs in the room. I looked over and there the both of them lay, on the sofa, curled up together asleep. Now was that precious or what of the Lord? I'm sorry, but there can be no coincidence here because things have been too bad for weeks to all of a sudden do a 180 degree turnabout immediately after we prayed for it. Thank you Lord!

11. Steer, 80.
12. Arthur T. Pierson, *George Müller of Bristol* (New York: The Baker and Taylor Co., 1899), 85.
13. Pierson, 81.

14. "The thief does not come except to steal, and to kill, and to destroy. I have come that they may have life, and that they may have it more abundantly" (John 10:10). Pierson, 373.
15. Sheets, *Intercessory Prayer*
16. "For this purpose the Son of God was manifested, that He might destroy the works of the devil" (1 John 3:8).
17. Hebrews 11:6
18. Roger Steer, *Delighted in God* (New York: Hodder & Stoughton, 1990).

WinePressPublishing
Your Book, Defined.
Since 1991.

To order additional copies of this book call:
1-877-421-READ (7323)
or please visit our Web site at
www.WinePressbooks.com

If you enjoyed this quality custom-published book,
drop by our Web site for more books and information.

www.winepresspublishing.com
"Your partner in custom publishing."